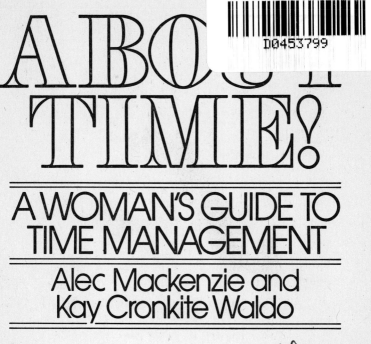

ABOUT TIME!

A WOMAN'S GUIDE TO TIME MANAGEMENT

Alec Mackenzie and Kay Cronkite Waldo

MC GRAW- HILL BOOK COMPANY

New York   St. Louis   San Francisco   Auckland

Bogotá   Guatemala   Hamburg   Johannesburg   Lisbon

London   Madrid   Mexico   Montreal   New Delhi

Panama   Paris   San Juan   São Paulo   Singapore

Sydney   Tokyo   Toronto

First McGraw-Hill Paperback edition, 1981

1 2 3 4 5 6 7 8 9 0 F G F G 8 7 6 5 4 3 2 1

LIBRARY OF CONGRESS CATALOGING IN PUBLICATION DATA
Mackenzie, R. Alec.
About time!
Includes index.
1. Women—Time management.   2. Housewives—
Time management. I. Waldo, Kay Cronkite, joint
author. II. Title.
HQ1221.M215 1981   640′.43′088042   80-21985
ISBN 0-07-044651-2 (pbk.)

Book design by Christine Aulicino

CONTENTS

PREFACE

Time presents problems to all of us:

    You can't save it and use it later.

    You can't elect not to spend it.

    You can't borrow it.

    You can't leave it. Nor can you retrieve it.

    You can't take it with you, either.

But . . .

    Time is always with you—and you can lose it, or *use* it. This book is for the active woman—a look at your time and, yes, your life. Time management is especially crucial for women. If you are married or single, and especially if you have children, you must cope with the demands of both your home and your career, whether you are an employed woman or an involved volunteer.

    To fulfill these time-consuming responsibilities, a woman has to become an expert manager of her time. If you want to function successfully, you must seek more efficient and effective ways to juggle your office and home routines.

Actually, a woman has to be a better manager of her time both on and off the job than most of her male peers. Women have traditionally carried the major responsibilities for the maintenance of the home in addition to their outside activities. In fact, as a woman, you need to be a master time planner merely to coordinate your life!

As you read this book you'll discover some things about yourself and your time you didn't know—and rediscover some you've known but just haven't thought about recently. For example, why do some days go so well, while others go so badly? On some days why do I get so *much* done . . . and on others so *little?* Why am I always running out of time? Why does delegation work at the office, but not at home? How *do* I prioritize? How do I match my tasks to my energy levels? How do I say no to unreasonable demands? How do I find time for *myself* ?

If these, and questions like them, are your problems, this book will help you solve them. Thousands of women around the world are using the techniques described in this book to help them find *their* way to better use of *their* time. If the techniques work for them, they can work for you!

So, good luck—and best wishes for successful management of your time *and* your life!

KAY CRONKITE WALDO   R. ALEC MACKENZIE
Kansas City, Missouri   *Greenwich, New York*

ABOUT TIME!

THE CHALLENGE

I always thought that Time Management was tying
mops to your feet so that when you get up to go to the
bathroom at night, you can be accomplishing
something.

ANNETTE MORGAN (1979)

Betty, the harried homemaker, races from preparing breakfast for her family to participating in the neighborhood car-
pool, attending a committee meeting, shopping for
groceries, on and on all day, while Norma, the account executive, nervously juggles her responsibilities at home with
a full-time job and out-of-town business trips. It's no wonder
that many women plead for MORE TIME.

As novelist May Sarton describes it, "trapped . . . one
did one's work against a steady barrage of demands, of
people . . . the fact was that the days of men were not in the
same way fragmented, atomized by indefinite small tasks.
There was such a thing as woman's work and it consisted

3

chiefly . . . in being able to stand constant interruption and keep your temper. Each single day she fought a war to get to her desk before her little bundle of energy had been dissipated, to push aside or cut through an intricate web of slight threads pulling her in a thousand directions—that unanswered letter, that telephone call. . . ."[1]

Time flies! I never have enough time! I'm running out of time! A familiar lament of today's active woman. Without realizing it, we usually talk about time as if it is something we can control or manipulate to our own liking. In reality time is a constant—there isn't any more of it. Each of us has all the time there is. We discover the paradox of time: Few people have enough, yet everyone has all there is!

If you have all the time there is, then you must shift gears and consider the real issue: How can you as an individual effectively manage the time you do have? Do you have a clear understanding of how you currently use your time? Do you assess and set priorities for yourself, and do you know how to say no to others and their demands in order to give yourself "free" time? Or do you race madly from one day to the next, feeling harried and out of control with no real sense of accomplishment? Learning to manage your time effectively is the key to living a less frantic and more satisfying life.

Time is a constant. As management philosopher Peter Drucker observed, "Time is the scarcest resource and unless it is managed nothing else can be managed."[2] And yet throughout our society there is evidence that the value of time is not recognized. Most organizations and businesses don't recognize the value of their managers' time. For example, the company may expect Lydia, the personnel direc-

---

[1] May Sarton, *Mrs. Stevens Hears the Mermaids Singing* (New York: Norton, 1975).

[2] Peter F. Drucker, "How to Be an Effective Executive," *Nation's Business*, April 1961.

tor, to sit in on the weekly marketing meetings when her time might be better spent developing that long-needed personnel manual. Or, Janet, as executive secretary, may still be typing all the form letters instead of having them prepared by the typing pool. Time, not money, is any company's most critical resource.

As an individual woman, time is your most critical resource, too. And the issue for you is *not* how to manage your time, but rather, how to manage yourself in relation to time. As you shift your thinking to recognizing that time management is really self-management, you can begin to glimpse the light at the end of the tunnel. You can examine and more clearly understand the psychological and sociological reasons for your time management difficulties and how you can apply new techniques and skills to enhance your effectiveness.

A Time and Success Formula

As new options open up for women, the demands on their time increase. Often the most difficult choices to be made for women today are between positive alternatives: Homemaking is satisfying, a career is fulfilling, more education is intriguing, and an active social life is fun! The individual woman can create for herself a unique combination of activities and a life-style that responds to both her own needs and the needs of those around her. She can create her own success formula.

What is success? The definition will vary for each of us. Furthermore, the meaning of success will vary for each of us at different stages in our individual lives. Perhaps a definition that most can agree on is that "Success = progressive realization of goals." To reach those goals requires that we manage our time in relation to them. An important part of that process is to understand the impact of our socialization as women on our attitudes toward time.

Female Socialization and Its Impact

Most women in American society have been conditioned to view their primary role as that of the nurturer, the one who is to be responsive to the needs of others. She is to be tuned in to the expectations of those around her and to view the needs of others as more important than her own. Consequently, to view one's own needs and time as equally valuable, and in some cases more valuable, is particularly difficult for many women. In a very real sense, the ability of a woman to manage her time is directly related to her sense of what it is to be a woman.

Reactive Rather Than Proactive

A woman has been conditioned to be reactive rather than proactive, to be in a passive state of readiness. She is conditioned to wait for a demand to be made to which she can respond rather than to take a proactive role in determining what demands can legitimately be made upon her and how to manage them. Just as the new female member of an agency board may agree to serve on committees which don't interest her rather than expressing a preference for ones she's really interested in, so may a secretary continue to use an out-of-date filing system to avoid recommending a different and more effective approach.

A woman is apt to feel that if she becomes more proactive, if she does take charge of her own life, she will lose her femininity . . . that somehow the more forceful and personally powerful she becomes, the less feminine she will be. So for many women there is an internal resistance to taking charge of their own time.

Pleasing Others

Another important factor in women's fear and concern about taking charge of their own lives is that many carry around a basic feeling of not being OK, some sense of not quite measuring up. As a consequence many women have learned that the only way to experience themselves as having personal worth is to win the approval of other people. As long as another person or other people are approving of her, then she's OK. If that approval is withdrawn in any way— either because she has challenged someone's opinion, disagreed on a particular point, or gotten angry—then she'll experience herself as being not OK. Consequently it is often more difficult for women in the business world, for example, to delegate responsibility, to be in charge of a staff, or to say no to someone. Even what seem to be simple kinds of communication are stumbling blocks because many women have been conditioned to please other people at almost any cost. If a woman has that much investment in other people and their opinions of her, it's obviously going to be more difficult for her to risk displeasure and rejection by being her own effective time manager.

At a psychological level, saying yes to yourself and no to others, even though rationally acceptable to a woman, may be disconcerting. A major goal for a woman is recognizing that a healthy balance in one's personality combines not only being aware and responsive to the demands of others but also being responsive to her own wants and needs.

Lacking Skills in Rational Thinking

Although women have been socialized to be "feeling" persons and to be tuned in to the needs of others, they've often not received childhood training in being rational and objective. Most women are much more "in touch" with their feelings (perhaps with the exception of anger) than with the "thinking" part of themselves, and time management is a *thinking* process.

An example of how this discrepancy occurs is illustrated by an experience of four-year-old twins, Susie and Johnnie. One day they are both outside playing while

Mommy is working in the kitchen. Pretty soon Susie comes running inside, crying. She's upset because the arm of her doll fell off. Mommy pulls Susie into her arms, caresses her, and tells her "Go ahead and cry, honey . . . I understand how you feel. . . . Now, let's put the dolly over on the counter and when Daddy comes home he'll fix it."

A few minutes later Johnnie comes running inside. He's crying because the wheel of his fire truck fell off. Mommy pats him on the head and says, "Now, Johnnie, don't cry, don't cry. Why don't you sit down and see if you can figure out how to put the wheel back on that fire truck?"

The messages to Susie and Johnnie are diametrically opposed. To Susie, the message that Mommy conveys is "Susie, it's OK to feel, to cry. Now, take whatever your problem is, put it aside, and soon a man will come and make it OK." The message to Johnnie is "Don't feel, don't cry. Now, sit down and figure out how to solve your problem." In simpler language, the message to Susie is "Feel, don't think." The message to Johnnie is "Think, don't feel."

No wonder that by the time men and women are adults, many men are less tuned in to their feelings and many women lack skill in thinking rationally and objectively. In order to evaluate her current use of time and to make constructive changes in managing her time, a woman must have rational and objective thinking skills.

Superwoman Syndrome

The socialization of women into nurturing and supporting roles has dramatically impacted the life of the employed woman, who usually views herself as having several full-time responsibilities—including not only her employment but also the maintenance of her home and family. Research indicates that employed women are still carrying the major load at home in addition to whatever their work responsibilities may be.

Because of the irrational fear that a woman may feel about becoming successful and, as a result, losing her femininity, she may attempt to become Superwoman—the successful businesswoman, immaculate housekeeper, loving wife, attentive mother, gracious hostess and gourmet cook—an unrealistic expectation and one that can produce high levels of tension and stress. For the woman who embraces this Superwoman mentality, the management of her time becomes a never-ending frustration. For many women, then, part of effective time management includes a recognition of these unrealistic expectations of herself and the development of a more rational set of values related to her activities and life-style.

For example, this process may involve assessing what her personal needs are for social relationships. What for her is a healthy balance between career, family, and other friendships and activities? Many women will say, "I just don't have time for any social life, clubs, sports, or hobbies. . . ." This is an unwise decision. Psychologists agree that to be a healthy, functioning person, a portion of one's time needs to be spent in "playing"—whether that be parties, sports, hobbies . . . whatever for us as individuals is an enjoyable diversion. Many women find that they need to schedule in their tennis or bridge just as they do a committee meeting or a doctor's appointment for their child. Although this scheduling of "play time" seems artificial, it may be necessary to establish an initial habit of taking her "fun" activities seriously. A survey of working women made by the National Commission on Working Women reports that lack of leisure time is viewed as a problem by over 50 percent of the women surveyed![3]

[3] Leslie Bennett, "When Homemaking Becomes Job No. 2," *The New York Times*, July 14, 1979.

Career Uncertainty

Women often feel the constraints of time because they are starting their careers later than many men, perhaps after having raised several children. Rather than having been on a focused career path since high school, they are at the ages of thirty-five or forty-five beginning to explore their career development. The frustration of needing to "catch up" combined with often inadequate assertive skills can create considerable anxiety for the individual woman. To deal with this anxiety, many women are learning that they can space their commitments, that their lives are to some extent episodic. Their priorities shift between childrearing, a career, more education, a new hobby—each taking precedence at different times in their lives.

Describing her experience, one successful woman now in her forties states, "In adult life studies (mostly of men) there is a 'hurry-up' for many men in their thirties when they realize that they still have things they want to accomplish, and 'time' is getting shorter. I have had the same experience. My twenties and early thirties was primarily a 'holding period,' or at least, time was not a factor. There seemed plenty of it.

"After a mid-life crisis (thirty-six—mine seemed to go on for years!), I became conscious that I needed to define goals more clearly, identify new goals, and set about accomplishing them."

An important part of effective time management *is* deciding what you really want to do with your life, what your priorities are, short- and long-term. A woman needs to shift her emphasis from "doing everything" to doing the *right* things, those activities which will maximize the use of her skills, resulting in a sense of fulfillment and accomplishment.

As described in Hennig and Jardim's book, *The Managerial Woman,* a woman may often have a different concept of time regarding her personal career strategy.[4] Where a man will make decisions based on not only the short-term payoff but, even more important, his long-term career goals, a woman often will not perceive long-term implications. She is more likely to make a "here and now" decision with far less consideration of how that specific decision will affect her career in the future.

Also, a woman may experience difficulty in managing time because her personal needs are not being met by the particular work in which she's involved. She may consequently be rebellious, procrastinating, or apathetic in her efforts. She may need to assess her effectiveness on her current job by considering what her work-related needs and values really are. Richard N. Bolles, in his book *The Three Boxes of Life,* suggests the following criteria for measuring the payoffs one receives from her current employment:

1. . . . I am able to keep busy.
2. . . . I am able to enjoy my work.
3. . . . I can achieve or accomplish something that has some meaning to it, for me.
4. . . . my work gives me a sense of power over others.
5. . . . my work is satisfying my need for affiliation . . . i.e., for relationships.
6. . . . my work fits in with my need to love and/or my need to be loved.[5]

Time management for a woman, then, is more than a technique or a series of techniques that she can layer on top of her personality and expect major change. To manage her time most effectively requires that she take an in-depth look

---

[4] Margaret Hennig and Anne Jardim, *The Managerial Woman* (Garden City, N.Y.: Anchor Press, 1977).

[5] Richard N. Bolles, *The Three Boxes of Life* (Berkeley, California: Ten Speed Press, 1978), pp. 304–326.

at her personality and what her experiences and socialization have been. Then she can understand more clearly how she may be blocking herself from managing her time effectively.

Some Pluses for Women!

In addition to the problems that many women encounter in time management, there are also some pluses that have resulted because of their socialization. Although there have been multiple demands made upon the lives of women in terms of family and societal pressures, many women have learned how to deal effectively with those multiple demands—the two-year-old needing to eat, the husband wanting help in finding a canceled check, and the telephone ringing, all at the same time. Most women have learned to deal with more than one person and/or situation at one time and to set priorities quickly. That ability is a key to effective time management.

In addition, because most women have been socialized to be particularly aware of their emotions, they are in touch with their moods and the varying energy levels that they experience during a day, a week, or a month. The more a woman can match a demand that is being made on her with an appropriate energy level, the more productive she will be. For example, if a woman's most highly energized time during the day is between nine and eleven in the morning, then—if she's aware—that can be the time she schedules major responsibilities. Also, if her lowest energy level is in the late afternoon, she can select the tasks which fit that lower energy level. All of this requires a close monitoring of herself which many women are more trained and comfortable in doing than are most men.

Your greatest strength as a woman may be that you have learned to be flexible, to adjust. Consequently, you are open to change.

Becoming a more effective manager of your time is a process of change, of learning more about yourself and considering new options for your life. Perhaps Ann Richards, a wife, mother, and elected official in Texas, best describes the growing self-understanding and openness to change of a woman in relationship to her time. She says:

The only important principle of time management that I am certain about is more philosophical than technical. Simply . . . you cannot do everything that everyone wants you to do at the time that they want you to do it. I have come to terms with the fact that my house will be messy, my child wrinkled, and that my husband will wash dishes, clean house, do the laundry, drive the children around, and go to the grocery store. I will not attend every reception that I am invited to attend, join every committee that wants me, take on any task that sounds interesting, or solve every problem that surfaces. . . .

And yet you can, by managing your time effectively, reach more of your goals in all the areas of your life.

The challenge is there . . . and so are the answers!

2

WHERE DOES YOUR TIME GO?

Without discipline there is no life at all.

KATHARINE HEPBURN

Time Management Is
Self-Management

Can time really be managed? Is the phrase *time management* a possibility . . . or is it a complete misstatement? The answer lies in the fundamental nature of time itself.

Perspectives on time vary and are full of surprises. The same period of time that seems to pass in a fleeting moment for one woman may take an eternity for another. One may be delightfully preoccupied, the other painfully bored. The seeming slowness or quickness of time passing does vary depending on one's current activity and attitude.

For most women there is never enough time to get everything done. For a few there does seem to be time enough—and therefore a lot less stress. Yet the days are the same for both. Each day has twenty-four hours—1440 minutes—no matter who or where you are. So not having enough time is an excuse, not a reason. Each woman has all there is.

And time moves at the same rate the world around. Seconds merge into minutes . . . minutes into hours. In reality, time never flies and never drags. It is the most inexorable and inelastic element in our existence. The only constant and totally predictable resource is the availability and movement of time. Paradoxically, it is also the least understood, poorest managed, most abused and misused of all our resources.

Why is this so? From the authors' experience this paradox results from a lack of awareness of the value of time and how easily it slips through our fingers. In short, we take time for granted. We *assume* we use it well without ever testing that assumption. It simply doesn't occur to us to ask such basic questions as "What is the best use of my time right now?" or "Was the result of a given effort *worth* the time it took?"

Have *you* asked either of these questions recently? Would you know how to answer them if you had? The answer, of course, is to know what you want to accomplish with your time in specific, measurable terms and to evaluate the results you actually achieved in terms of their cost in time.

We say we "haven't enough time." Yet we know that everyone has all there is. Clearly the problem isn't time but how we use it. The issue with respect to time is therefore not how we manage *it*, but how we manage *ourselves* with respect to time. Time management is really self-management.

Log Your Time

To determine an individual's areas in greatest need of self-management, the most powerful tool is the time log. After all, how can you manage your time if you don't know where it's going? Many carefully conducted studies from around the world confirm the tremendous disparity between where people *think* their time is going . . . and where their time logs show it actually goes.

A time log is a simple listing and analysis of every activity during a given period of time. Through plotting carefully your use of time on the time log, you get a much clearer picture of where your time is actually going and whether you are making maximum use of the time available.

Daily Time Log

The instructions below should be followed in detail to ensure that the Daily Time Log (Figure 1) is of maximum value to you. If you need additional shorthand symbols so you can record items quickly, make up a few you understand at a glance. (Upon completion of your time log, compare it with the sample log in the Appendix, page 220.)

INSTRUCTIONS FOR TAKING DAILY TIME LOG

1. Enter name, date, and goals.
2. Record each activity as the day progresses. Record all interruptions, their source and reason. Give as much detail as possible.
3. Set a priority on each action, so that you can check back at the end of the day to see how much time was spent on top priority work.
4. Comment on each action with a view to future improvements. Try to note suggestions for making these improvements.
5. Keep logs for a minimum of three days; one week is preferable. Allow time at end to analyze your logs.
6. Use signs and abbreviations; Phone call out: c→ Phone call in: →c, etc.

Figure 1

DAILY TIME LOG

Name: _____   Date: _____

Daily Goals: Deadline   Deadline

(1) _____ _____   (4) _____ _____

(2) _____ _____   (5) _____ _____

(3) _____ _____   (6) _____ _____

Priority: **1**—Most Import.; **2**—Less Import.; **3**—Routine Detail; **4**—Least Import.

Time	Activity	Time Used	Prior	Comment/Disposition

Questions for Analyzing Your Time Log
After making a time log for yourself, it's important to analyze it carefully. Only in that way will you clarify your
strengths and weaknesses in managing your time. The following questions will aid you in your evaluation.

1. Did you have a plan for each day with clear priorities in
   writing?
   > How long did it take you to get around to the
   > number-one priority for the day?
   > How many times did you permit yourself to be inter-
   > rupted before finishing it?
2. Were you doing the right job at the right time?
   > What did you do that should not have been done at
   > all?
   > Could it have been done later?
   > Could it have been delegated? To whom?
3. What could be done in a better way?
   > Faster?
   > More simply?
   > In less detail?
   > With better results?
4. Concerning interruptions:
   > How are you interrupted most often? (telephone,
   > visitors, meetings, crises, self, boss, team, clients,
   > children, neighbors, spouse?)
   > How often?
   > For how long?
   > How important were the interruptions?
   > How long does it take to recover—to get back on the
   > track?
   > How many interrupted tasks were left unfinished at
   > the end of the day?
   > How much time do you spend responding to crises
   > that could have been anticipated and prevented and
   > in doing things you could have delegated?

5. Concerning contacts/communications with others:
   How important? (Is time spent in accordance with your real priorities?)
   Who (with right person?)
   How often?
   How long?
6. To what extent did you reach your goals?

Why and When to Log

Reasons for taking a time log vary from the general desire to discover where one's time is going to the specific target of analyzing a particular timewaster such as interruptions from telephone calls and drop-in visitors. Logs may be taken in at least three different ways for as many different purposes:

1. *The periodic time log,* quarterly, or at least semiannually, will at the outset enable you to identify your time-use patterns and timewasters. Upon repetition it will enable you to measure your progress in controlling your timewasters and will serve as a reinforcement to prevent falling back into your old bad habits.
2. *The targeted time log* permits detailed analysis of a particular timewaster. Example: a log of all phone calls or drop-in visitors noting person, frequency, duration, purpose, and relative priority of subject discussed.
3. *The continuous, daily time log* provides a powerful self-disciplining tool that alerts you immediately to time being wasted and encourages instant corrective action.

A very active woman who discovered the continuous time log to be her best tool for enhancing self-discipline in managing her time said:

I've taken a time log daily since taking your seminar four years ago. It tells me the moment a day starts slipping out of control, and I *automatically* take corrective measures. I dislike writing down

activities I *know* are a waste of time. I'm in meetings every day so
many entries are short. My log rarely exceeds one page. Since I
normally enter the activity *while* it's going on . . . a call, a visit, or
a meeting, for example . . . it rarely takes more than five minutes
to make the entries for the entire day. Of course, I use shorthand
signals and abbreviations too. I'll never stop taking a log. It's the
most powerful tool for self management I've ever discovered. It
has improved my productivity enormously.

Benefits of a Time Log
The benefits of taking a time log are surprisingly numerous.
When we ask seminar attendees what they learned from
taking their preseminar logs, the answers vary from "how
poorly I was managing my time" to "I noticed that I did a
lot better *because* I was keeping track of how I was using my
time." Most commonly they respond "I was appalled at the
incredible number of interruptions . . . I looked at the time
I spend in meetings and asked myself what I'm really getting
out of them . . . I'm my own biggest problem because I
keep interrupting myself at the slightest excuse. . . . Most
of my time is spent reacting rather than initiating. . . . It
seems that I have less control over my time than others do.
. . I can see that having set priorities for the day makes it a
lot easier to resist interruptions of lower priority."

To summarize, a time log helps you to:

1. Discover where your time is *really* going. It isn't going
   where you think.
2. Identify time-use patterns and timewasters which are
   difficult to identify in any other way . . . or to accept if
   told about them by others.
3. Analyze time use by category and priority of activity.
4. Take corrective measures, many of which are painfully
   obvious, such as controlling interruptions or organizing your desk to aid in retrieving documents.
5. Check progress in order to avoid regressing into old
   bad habits.

6. Provide reinforcement to ensure that new and better work habits are maintained.

How NOT to Log Time

Very few people take valid time logs on their first attempt. From thousands of logs we have reviewed, it is possible to identify the most common mistakes of inexperienced time loggers.

Too general terms. Comments are too general, not specific or detailed enough to permit analysis. Example: "Talked with Gloria James" instead of "Answered Gloria James's questions re Project X." General, nonspecific entries prevent identification of the priority of the activity, and, therefore, any analysis of the effectiveness of the use of that particular time span is impossible. Evaluating the appropriate allocation of time to relative priorities is one of the key objectives of taking a time log.

Fixed intervals. Many time logs are divided into fifteen-minute or half-hour intervals with only one line provided for entries during each interval. This necessitates omitting entries when more than one activity occurs in any given time frame. What will invariably be omitted are the short interruptions, usually those by telephone or drop-in visitors, which are among the most serious of all time wasters. They break the continuity of thought and destroy concentration and momentum. Furthermore, studies indicate that it can take three times as long to recover from an interruption as it takes to endure it. So the importance of providing space for each interruption or change in activity is clear. Rather than prescribing only one entry for each fixed quarter- or half-hour interval, the authors recommend omitting time intervals so that all interruptions as well as normal activity changes can be logged.

Skipping less important entries. Most of us have an ego need to look good on paper. This results in tending to record the more important activities and to stretch the time actually spent on them. When suddenly aware that no entries have been made for half an hour or more, the temptation to fill in the log with some high-sounding phrase like "planning" is great. This defeats the number-one objective of the log, which is to tell you the true picture of where your time really is going.

Random, not continuous, entries. When you wait until a "convenient time" to make entries in the log, you are simply inviting inaccuracy, since no memory is that good. Studies of managers' use of time indicate they are interrupted on the average every eight minutes all day long. That accounts for a minimum of approximately eight different activities per hour, assuming the person never succeeded in returning to the task which was interrupted. Observers estimate that this happens less than half the time. So you could be trying to recall many different activities every time you wait only an hour to make your entries. To wait half a day, or an entire day, reduces the whole exercise to the ridiculous. It makes any effort to analyze how time really *was* spent or the effectiveness of its utilization futile.

Failure to record category and priority of activities. Women sometimes diligently record nearly every activity for the day but forget to categorize them and to assign them a priority. This defeats the log's most important purpose, which is to determine the effectiveness of the time allocated to the relative priorities.

Failure to analyze time-use patterns and to take corrective action. The ultimate purpose of the log is to discover *where* your time is going and to analyze it so that you can *take corrective action*. To go to the effort of recording all activities for three days, a week or two weeks, and then leave them without review, analysis, and corrective action is to commit a serious waste of time in the name of saving time.

Getting into the Habit of Managing Your Time

Self-management involves habits—breaking bad work habits and developing new ones. This is not so simple a task, as anyone who has ever tried to stop smoking—or eating or being late or forgetting—will confirm.

Will James, the noted psychologist, called habit "the flywheel of society, its most precious conserving agent." "The great thing," he urged, "is to make our nervous system our ally instead of our enemy. We must automate and habituate, as early as possible, as many useful actions as we can, and guard against growing into ways that are disadvantageous as we guard against the plague. The more of the details of our daily life we can hand over to the effortless custody of automation, the more our higher powers of the mind will be set free for their proper work."[1]

The *most serious* problem in managing your time concerns neither identifying your timewasters nor developing and implementing solutions, important as they may be. Most of these deal with obvious steps such as having calls and visitors screened or setting deadlines on major tasks. These are neither difficult to conceive nor to implement. But the problem comes in *persisting*—sticking with it.

SIX STEPS FOR DEVELOPING GOOD
TIME MANAGEMENT HABITS

1. *Recognize the difficulty.* Longtime bad habits aren't broken easily.
2. *Develop a better way.* The best defense is a good offense. The easiest way to break a bad habit is to replace it.

[1] William James, "Making Habits Work for You," *Readers' Digest*, August 1967.

3. *Launch the new habit strongly*. Weak initiatives die quickly.
4. *Go public*. By announcing it you become committed.
5. *Repeat it often*. Take every opportunity to practice and reinforce it.
6. *Allow no exceptions*. Exceptions quickly become the rule, and you'll be back in your old bad habits.

FACING UP TO YOUR TIMEWASTERS

Time must be seen as a valuable gift and tool to use to accomplish our priorities, be they social change, personal fulfillment, or "nothing today." Time is one element that an individual can have power over.

MARILYN FOWLER (1980)

To manage yourself in relationship to time involves a high degree of self-understanding. As described in the preceding chapter, when logging your time, you need to be honest with yourself so that you're recording accurately and completely the way you *actually* use time rather than the way you believe you should. You also need to recognize that many timewasters are *self-induced*. In many instances, *you* are generating the timewasting activity; it's not being imposed on you by outside persons or circumstances.

Top Timewasters for Women

To more clearly understand how you, as an individual woman, compare with large numbers of other women in managing your time, consider the following profiles. These rankings are a composite of three different surveys in which groups of female secretaries, homemakers, and managers identified their top timewasters. Their rankings are compared with the worldwide ranking of all managers. Although there are some obvious differences in rankings among the three categories of women due to differing daily activities—as well as to the fact that these are random, not scientific, samplings—there are also some striking similarities.

Timewaster Defined

In seminars where these timewaster rankings have been compiled, the word *timewaster* has been defined to mean anything preventing you from achieving your objectives most effectively. "Effectiveness" means achieving maximum results with minimum cost (in our case, time).

Select Your Own Timewasters

As you reflect on your own activities and life-style, take a few minutes to jot down your top ten timewasters, using the above list as a way to stimulate your thinking. (If you've completed a time log for yourself, that provides a valuable source of information about your specific timewasters.)

Now rank your timewasters in the order of their impact on your life, number one being the biggest timewaster for you, number two the next . . . until you have your personal profile completed.

After finishing the rankings, go back through the list and put a check mark by those timewasters which are self-induced—the ones you have generated for yourself. As you read this book, write down possible solutions.

Discovering your timewasters is the key to managing yourself in relationship to time!

FOUR CATEGORIES OF TIMEWASTERS[1]

TIMEWASTER	WORLD-WIDE ALL MANAGERS	WOMEN MANAGERS	HOME-MAKERS	SECRE-TARIES
Telephone interruptions	1	1	2	1
Crisis management/ shifting priorities	2		6	3
Lack objectives, priorities, planning	3	9	5	2
Drop-in visitors	4	2	9	9
Ineffective delegation	5	5	1	15
Attempting too much at once	6		3	5
Meetings	7	8	17	
Personal disorganization/cluttered desk	8	12	12	19
Inability to say no	9	10	10	
Lack self-discipline	10		21	
Procrastination/ indecision	11		8	16
Untrained, inadequate staff	12		13	
Incomplete, delayed information	13	7		
Paperwork, red tape, reading	14			11
Leaving tasks unfinished	15		7	18
Unclear communication and instructions	16			13
Understaffed	17	6		
Confused responsibility and authority	18	4		
Socializing (See Telephone and Visitors)	19	10		9
Chauffeuring children			4	
Excessive errands				6
Interruptions by boss				7
Disorganized boss				8

[1] These are categories and figures tabulated by Alec Mackenzie in his seminars.

BLAMING OTHERS.   When women are asked to identify their timewasters either at work or at home, they usually think first of those that can be blamed on others, such as interruptions by phone, drop-in visitors, unexpected crises, urgent meetings, shifting priorities by others, and so on. After some thought and discussion, however, a different type of timewaster begins to emerge: that kind that can be blamed only on oneself. These include procrastination, personal disorganization, lack of planning, poor communication, failure to anticipate, ineffective delegation, indecision, and failure to follow up.

The difference in these two lists suggests one of the major problems for women as businesswomen, homemakers, volunteer coordinators, or students: lack of awareness of your *own* real timewasters. You will discover that most timewasters are self-generated. And you may be surprised to discover the extent to which other timewasters, those you tend to blame on others, can be controlled or at least influenced by you—with very little effort in many cases.

HER SECRETARY WAS THE PROBLEM.   A female volunteer coordinator in Chicago, for example, complained to us that her secretary was a real problem. The coordinator had almost decided to make a change, but first wanted to confirm her decision. She was sure, however, that a better secretary would solve most of her concerns.

In the view of the secretary, her *manager*, the volunteer coordinator, was the problem. The manager never took time to brief her secretary, so the secretary was left to guess what were her boss's goals and plans for the day. When the coordinator did communicate, it was usually fast, unclear, and incomplete. The boss criticized the least oversight and never seemed to notice when things went well.

By the end of the seminar, the coordinator had a list of action items, most of which dealt with ways in which she could cooperate better with her secretary. She now saw clearly that the major problem had been herself. Some weeks later she observed that she'd failed to appreciate that she had a really top secretary all along. She'd simply not known how to allow her secretary to help her in the ways she could, and would have liked! Meanwhile, the secretary had been understandably demotivated and ready to quit her job in hopes of finding a better boss.

"TO SEE OURSELVES . . .". A division president of a major food corporation and his secretary had an equally dramatic experience. In a time management seminar for manager-secretary teams, each person was asked to identify, from a list of forty, his or her top ten timewasters, and then, on a separate sheet, to identify the top ten timewasters of the partner. When the president and his secretary exchanged their lists, each was astounded to see that "Not Listening" was the top choice of each of them—for the *other* person! "Ah," said Robert Burns, "to see ourselves as others see us. . . ."

Self-Generated Timewasters
Not Setting Deadlines
Every major task needs to be deadlined. Overlooking the power of deadlines is one of the most common and most costly mistakes we make. The prevailing reasons for not setting deadlines are similar to the reasons why managers resist setting objectives. Not wanting to be subject to accountability for an objective *or* a deadline causes most of us to hold back. The fear of failure and the desire to maintain independence and freedom of action are also powerful forces which militate against imposing deadlines on ourselves. Simple failure to recognize their importance means that the thought of deadlining may never occur to some of us.

The well-known Parkinson's Law advises that work tends to expand to fill the time available. In other words, give a person all day to finish a task and, in all probability, the task will take all day, even if it *could* have been completed much faster. Hence the wisdom of setting deadlines . . . to prevent jobs from taking much longer than they should. Most women acknowledge, for example, that they can clean a room in two hours if they have an important luncheon meeting scheduled. If, however, the day is more flexible, the same woman may spend three to four hours giving the same room a comparable cleaning.

Care must be taken to ensure that deadlines are *reasonable*. A deadline that allows much more time than is needed encourages wasted time and ineffective performance. On the other hand, an unrealistic deadline allowing too little time creates stress, pressure, haste, mistakes, and frustration. One way to know if your current deadline is reasonable is to have time-logged similar tasks in the past. You can refer to those logs and set your present deadline accordingly.

Not only do effective people impose deadlines on themselves to optimize their utilization of time and to ensure achievement of results, they also *induce others* to set deadlines—those working for them as well as those working with them. "When can you have that for me?" is a typical question of such a manager.

Procrastination

The human tendency to procrastinate provides an interesting window into the subject of self-discipline. That it takes self-discipline to resist putting things off is obvious. Less obvious is the pervasive nature of this human characteristic. The humor surrounding the subject attests to its universality. An example of this humor appeared on the wall of a supervisor in an electronics firm:

I'M GOING TO STOP PUTTING THINGS OFF read the top line of the sign in large, bold letters. Below, in smaller letters, it read:

"Starting tomorrow."

Below those two words, in tiny letters, appeared the word:

maybe.

We are told the National Association of Procrastinators has over 15,000 members. Its financial affairs have never been on a solid footing, however, since only 3500 have gotten around to paying their dues. And speaking of getting around to things, a few years ago thousands of *round* buttons appeared with the word TUIT printed on them . . . "for those who've never gotten around to it."

One time-management consultant coined the phrase *creative procrastination*, suggesting certain activities may be better accomplished in the end by putting them off for the time being. Some matters need time to mature or to permit reflection. Judgment is required to distinguish between matters that will benefit from procrastination and those that will not.

TO MASTER PROCRASTINATION. Causes of procrastination range from preferring to do pleasant or easy tasks first to fearing failure on complex or difficult assignments and from failure to set deadlines to not having enough to do.

To master procrastination you should first ask: Of all the things I *could* do, what do I *really need* to get done? By listing these goals or objectives under three categories, "Must, Should, and Could," you have already determined your priorities (Musts), which are really rank-ordered objectives. Equally important, you have determined what *not* to do, unless and until the "musts" and "shoulds" have been accomplished. Dr. David Mackenzie of the University of Massachusetts observed, in reflecting on his utilization of time, that the most critical step in managing his time was to decide, among the myriad of choices, what things should *not* be done because time simply did not permit them. After eliminating those things for which there was no time, he found the decision of what to do had, in effect, been made.

Next you should set deadlines on the "musts" to ensure that you will take them seriously and do them first instead of putting them off. Then go public: Commit yourself by announcing your deadlines and enlist the aid of others— an associate, a spouse, a secretary—to ensure that you do them.

Finally, get number one done first! Don't put it *off*. Put it *first*. Then, if nothing else gets done, you have completed the most important item and can strike it from your list. Many women in our studies who mentioned the use of deadlines commented on the psychological boost derived from marking off the most important task for the day from their list.

Indecision

One of the authors was told by his boss, president of a foundation, that the boss had registered him for a decision-making course. The boss had found the course of great value and thought the author would also. The author expressed surprise that anyone would need to attend a *course* on how to make a decision. (How could one be vice-president of a foundation and *not* be able to make a decision!) The course, five days in length, turned out to be one of the biggest "eye-openers" in the author's experience.[2] It had never occured to him that there was a rational process for making sound decisions which could correct most of the common shortcomings in decision-making. In fact, he'd never thought seriously about the shortcomings—or even identified them, for that matter. (One should distinguish, of

[2] Sponsored by Kepner, Tregoe and Associates, Princeton, New Jersey.

course, between indecision and deciding *not* to decide or proceed.)

EIGHT STEPS TO RATIONAL DECISIONS[3]

1. Define the decision or problem. (A problem well defined is half solved.)
2. Establish objectives for the decision or problem. (These are essential for choosing the best among alternative courses of action.)
3. Collect and collate critical facts. (Don't waste time gathering irrelevant, uncritical data.)
4. Develop the most viable alternatives and rate their relative effectiveness in achieving each of the objectives.
5. Identify and assess potential negative consequences of each alternative. (Ask "What could go wrong if this alternative were chosen?" Assess relative seriousness and probability of each potential consequence.)
6. Select best alternative based on most effective accomplishment of objectives and least negative consequences.
8. Monitor progress and take timely corrective action for deviations.

The inability to decide may be caused by fear of mistakes, uncertainty, lack of confidence, and a number of other factors relating to self-assurance and ego needs. Perhaps one of the most common causes is simple lack of awareness. As with any number of other personal characteristics, we may be totally unaware of our hesitance, vacillation, and indecisiveness until someone in a position to know counsels us, or a time log reveals it to us. We may also be unaware of the benefits of fast decisions, when they are appropriate. Not only do they provide a competitive time advantage where this is a factor, but they also provide more time to take corrective action if they should prove wrong.

---

[3] Adapted from the KTA "decision analysis process."

Decisiveness, along with willingness to take initiative, ranks
high on almost all lists of effective time management characteristics.

Leaving Tasks Unfinished

The following vignette about leaving tasks unfinished bears
repeating for a number of reasons. First, it's often in humor
that we glimpse the truth. Second, it applies to most of us
and will be recognized by almost everyone as a common,
everyday experience. Third, its lessons will escape us if we
fail to read it thoughtfully:

Marge has been asked to review last month's project report. As she
starts to do so, the telephone rings. It's someone asking about an
upcoming meeting schedule. So as she finds the schedule on her
desk, she sees that the morning mail has arrived. She stops to scan
the mail and begins reading a letter describing a new product which
could add considerably to the organization's efficiency. She sets
aside the meeting schedule, reads the letter more carefully, and
starts for the purchasing office to discuss it. On the way she passes
the cafeteria, smells the coffee brewing . . . so she decides to take
a break and have a roll and coffee. During the morning so far,
Marge has yet to complete a single task—she's accomplished nothing.

What are some of the causes of Marge's plight? Is she
drifting aimlessly because she has no clear objectives, priorities, or deadlines facing her? Does she perhaps have a difficult task she wants to avoid? Could it be that she has so
many unfinished tasks cluttering her desk that she really
can't face them? After all, there's always another day. Or is
she simply a very social creature who enjoys contact with
people and unconsciously gravitates to them rather than her
job? Maybe she doesn't believe in setting deadlines so she
feels no "sense of urgency" about getting on with her work.

With many of us there is a simple lack of self-
discipline, of determination to complete tasks. Dr. John

Mee, one of the deans of American management, called this "lacking compulsion to closure" in his excellent analysis of the problem. Most people seem to welcome interruptions—any break in the old routine. Being "interruption-prone," they fail to recognize the strong likelihood that they will not return to the task which has been interrupted. Once the concentration and momentum have been broken it is likely that one more task will be left unfinished.

The *most powerful antidote* to leaving tasks unfinished is the use of deadlines. If all major tasks are deadlined and announced, commitment and a compulsion to complete tasks results. The consequent sense of obligation is a powerful force for task completion.

Women who tell of success in completing tasks, so vital to the "dual-career woman," speak often of rewarding themselves *after* important though unpleasant tasks are accomplished. Rewards referred to by such successful women range from the minor (a cup of coffee) to the major (a significant pleasure trip). Getting and staying organized also plays an important role in preventing the interruptions which would otherwise be used as excuses for diversions into more pleasant activities. The screening of interruptions serves a similar vital role in aiding the continuity of concentration to permit completion of tasks. Finally, keeping your priorities visible (to serve as constant reminders) goes a long way toward warding off the temptations to leave unpleasant tasks before their completion.

Inability to Say No

"I've always wanted to know," said the politician, "a word which sounds like 'Yes' but more or less means 'No.'" The inability to say no—this powerful little two-letter word—has long afflicted not only politicians but people in all walks of life. Women in particular often desire to win approval and acceptance (the "pleasing others" syndrome). In addition, many have a normal humanitarian instinct to help others. They also may be afraid of offending the person asking for assistance, or they simply may be totally unaware of their inability to say no until their problems achieve a critical proportion where self-assessment becomes mandatory or some friend is candid with them.

A false sense of obligation assails many women who seem to feel that a request from anyone, no matter how unreasonable, must be legitimate or it would not be made. Along with this false sense of obligation there may be guilt feelings for having appeared to be unhelpful on previous occasions.

You may often have difficulty saying no when you lose sight of your own priorities, or don't have clear objectives in the first place. Then it becomes very difficult to decline seemingly reasonable requests of others. Without question, one of the best reasons for saying no to unreasonable demands is prior commitment to your own priorities. When these are absent, weak excuses seem to dissolve and you wind up saying yes, thereby letting others, in effect, set your priorities for you!

The timid approach of starting off with excuses in the hope of building up to a no rarely works. There seem to be answers for all excuses. As each excuse disappears, the ultimate yes becomes more certain.

So how do you say no when it ought to be said, and without offending? These four steps will work almost every time:

1. *Listen* . . . to show interest and understanding of the request.
2. Then *say no* immediately . . . to avoid building up false hopes.
3. *Give reasons* . . . so the refusal will be understood.
4. *Offer alternatives* if possible . . . to evidence good faith.

Women would do well to print these four underlined imperatives on a three-by-five card and tape it to their telephones.

One woman who followed these guidelines was the top salesperson in a very successful insurance agency in the Midwest. The manager of the agency took one of the authors to see her office the evening prior to a seminar for the office staff. "And here," he said, "is our top performer's office. She leaves on time. Her desk is clear. And I want you to see a sign over her telephone behind her desk." The sign read: **YOUR FRIENDS AND LOVED ONES WISH YOU WOULD SAY NO.** This woman has mastered the art of saying no. She worked no overtime, was well organized, kept her priorities in front of her at all times, refused to let interruptions and less important diversions distract her—*and* was the *top* producer in the agency!

Some women recognize that they are not always prepared with a ready reason for refusal when requests of doubtful importance are made. They effectively buy a little time by saying, "Let me think it over. If I can I'll let you know."

We must recognize that a reputation for saying yes does not guarantee anything but the certainty of more requests. The woman who knows how to say no, and who does so at appropriate times, will be getting more of the right things done and also have the respect of others.

Robert Updegraff, in his classic book, *All the Time You Need*,[4] summed up the case for saying no:

Over the years I have listened to people complain about not having the time for things they ought to do or would like to do. And I've discovered that many of them suffer from a common trouble: they are timid about using the greatest time-saving word in the English language, the little two-letter word "No."

[4] Robert R. Updegraff, *All The Time You Need* (Englewood Cliffs, N.J.: Prentice-Hall, 1958).

4

MANAGEMENT WORKS! AT THE OFFICE AND AT HOME

"There's nothing half so real in life as the things
you've done," she whispered. "Inexorably,
unalterably *done*."

MARGARET AYER BARNES (1931)

Women have not traditionally viewed themselves as managers. The word *management* itself conjures up images of a middle-aged man in a gray flannel suit making long-distance phone calls behind a mahogany desk in a plushly carpeted corner office! Times are changing, though. Women are not only assuming more positions of management in the worlds of business and government but are also recognizing their roles as managers at home and in the volunteer sector.

Management Principles and Their Applications

For several decades Larry Appley[1] was perhaps the best-known and most effective advocate of professional management in the world. In many films and in countless sessions with senior executives around the world he discussed the principles of *planning, organizing, staffing, directing, controlling, communicating,* and *decision making*.

A little-known conviction of Appley's was that the application of those principles in the home was equally as effective as at work. One of the authors conducted with Appley a management course for presidents and, simultaneously, another management course for their wives. All speakers addressed both sessions, and they expressed surprise on two counts. First, the speakers were surprised at the quality and intensity of the cross-examinations to which the wives subjected them. In addition, they felt that their sessions with the wives were more challenging and demanding than the one with the presidents. Finally, they expressed surprise at the almost total application of their presentations to the management of the home.

Typical applications of the seven managerial functions[2] in the home and at work are shown in the following chart:

APPLICATIONS OF MANAGEMENT PRINCIPLES

	HOME	OFFICE
Planning	A well-planned vacation will be far more likely to be an all-around success than one left to chance.	A performance evaluation program that is well planned will be far more likely to succeed than one that is not.

[1] Former President of the American Management Association.

[2] R. Alec Mackenzie, "The Management Process in 3D," *Harvard Business Review*, November–December 1969.

APPLICATIONS OF MANAGEMENT PRINCIPLES (*cont.*)

	HOME	OFFICE
Organiz-ing	Bills, correspondence, and important documents are much less likely to get lost if a desk and file are well organized and items are disposed of whenever possible on first handling.	Job descriptions which list expected outcomes in key result areas enhance the probability of achieving desired results.
Staffing	The selection of home machinery based upon availability of a given company's qualified service personnel enhances performance of machinery.	The quality of the selection, orientation, and training programs for new employees will directly affect production.
Directing	(Delegating) The art of delegating to rebellious children requires great managerial skill, and is far more likely to succeed if done professionally.	Since "managing" is defined as "achieving objectives through others," anyone who cannot delegate successfully cannot manage by definition!
	(Motivating) Congratulating a child on getting to play a couple of Little League innings will be more motivating than criticism for failure to get a hit.	Look to the challenges and satisfactions of tasks you assign as long-range motivators. Money is a "satisfier" with short-range results.
	(Coordinating) With children and parents all actively involved in various organizational and school activities, coordination of transportation	Among the major benefits of periodic staff meetings is the coordination of critical activities to ensure their timeliness and unity of effort.

APPLICATIONS OF MANAGEMENT PRINCIPLES (*cont.*)

	HOME	OFFICE
	with family and friends is essential to avoid a nightmare.	
Controlling	Tasks in the home are much more likely to be accomplished on a timely basis if they are listed for the day and the weekend under each person's name in a place that is visible to all.	Effective screening of phone calls and drop-in visitors conserves time for the manager while often achieving better and faster results for the person phoning or dropping in.
Communicating	Management experts rate the average adult only 25% effective at listening. Marital experts say spouses rate *each other* much lower. Yet far more time is spent listening than in any of the three other key communicating activities (talking, reading, and writing).	One of many key problems in effective delegation is failure to ensure that instructions have been clearly understood. Given our low average effectiveness in listening, it appears that three times as many instructions are misunderstood as are clearly understood. Effective managers ask that key instructions be restated to ensure understanding.
Decision making	Many decisions at home are postponed simply because deadlines have not been set. Set deadlines for key decisions which affect more than one member of the family.	Upward delegation is a common phenomenon in every organization. Effective managers refuse to make decisions which their subordinates should make.

Note that nearly all of the examples above are readily transferable between office and home. This illustrates that while specific applications of the principles and functions of management may vary from one office to another or from one home to another, their universal application in general cannot be disputed.

The reason for this is that a "principle" is a rule of conduct, a standard, a guideline for predicting results in given situations. And the fundamental rules remain the same even though their specific interpretation may vary depending upon circumstances.

Consequently, well-*planned* activities will achieve better results at home as well as at work. Getting and staying well *organized* allows for more effective time utilization and reduces overall personal stress. Choosing the *right people* to work with or from whom to buy equipment can affect performance dramatically, whether the office typewriter *or* the toaster at home is malfunctioning. When a team member or a family member is highly *motivated* or the beneficiary of effective *delegation*, each will perform with better results. When we fail to *coordinate* the plans for the day and the week with the team or family members the results are left to chance, and it can be predicted with near certainty that something will go wrong and a mini-crisis may develop.

Larry Appley appears to have coined the phrase "People do what you inspect, not what you expect." Of course it is possible to overdo the checking up on the performance of others. Overcontrol is a classic demotivator. Still, every homemaker and every office person has had the chilling experience of discovering, when it's too late to take corrective action, that a person to whom a critical action has been delegated has not followed through! *Provisions for ensuring that critical actions are carried out (control)* range from simple reminder phone calls or memos to regular progress reports at predetermined intervals.

Problems in *communication* arise in the home, in the office, and in virtually every activity that involves more than one person. They may include that argument with your son about straightening up his room before leaving for school, the conflict in the committee meeting about how much funding to provide for the service project, or the misunderstanding at the office over which supervisor is to set the project deadlines. Good interpersonal communication can be one of the greatest pleasures in living, while poor communication can be debilitating.

And finally, there is *decision making*, about which few adults, in *or* out of the business world, know very much.[3] Would anyone suggest that any fewer decisions are made in a busy home than in a busy office? Or that they are less consequential, especially when they involve matters like buying and financing a house or a car or perhaps which surgeon and hospital to select for open-heart surgery? And how rational *is* the process of deciding whether or not to change jobs because of an unexpected offer, or the selection of a key assistant from among the final four candidates? Yet the fundamentals of the rational process of decision making suggest that *any* decision or choice among alternative courses of action must involve certain critical steps.[4] For example, the gathering of relevant facts is vital and a prerequisite to evaluating alternative decisions in a given situation. Thus, the number of bedrooms in each prospective house, or the years of relevant experience each candidate has will be vital facts in two of the more common decisions faced by homemakers (choosing a new home) and managers (selecting a new employee).

[3] Articles and seminars on the subject notwithstanding.
[4] Charles Kepner and Benjamin B. Tregoe, *The Rational Manager* (New York: McGraw-Hill, 1965).

Managing the Home—A Transferable
Experience

Surprising to most women managers is the extent to which their experience as homemakers qualifies them to be excellent managers in business, volunteer organizations, or wherever they find themselves. When the initial surge of women into the work force reached significant proportions, many states set up counseling agencies to help them assess their own capabilities against the opportunities they sought. This was thought necessary because of the low self-image many women had of their own experience and capabilities. Review of their experience in *managing* households and volunteer activities, along with the requisite skills involved, radically altered the perception of many of these women.

In our judgment the home presents practically all of the management challenges of most offices. Indeed, in many respects it may present more difficult ones—for which no preparatory courses are offered, no management seminars conducted, no weekly or monthly digests of how to cope *managerially* are readily available.

In the following chapters we will address a variety of managerial skills. You will find them of significant value regardless of your particular activities or life-style, for they will cite example after example of practical steps toward solving the seemingly complex problems of managing, including getting things done through others. The universality of these principles and functions of management will become apparent. They are the same, whether you are managing an office or a home.

PLANNING—
THE PLACE TO START

This shall be my parting word—know what you want
to do—then do it. Make straight for your goal and go
undefeated in spirit to the end.

ERNESTINE SCHUMANN-HEINK (1935)

One of the surest distinctions between people who manage
time well and those who don't is whether or not they are
certain of their goals and their objectives. At times you've
noticed someone who seems too relaxed for a situation—
obviously not intent on accomplishing the task at hand. You
may have thought, "She doesn't seem to have very much to
do" or "I wish *I* had time like that!" Chances are that this
person doesn't have clear-cut objectives. She doesn't know
"where she's going."

Other times you've noticed someone who's alert in
situations, interested in what's going on, ready with a ques-

tion as to what comes next, not afraid to toss out a suggestion or to volunteer some initiative, if that's what's needed. About this person you think, "She's really with it" or "She always seems to know where she's going." Chances are she does.

From early childhood you've heard ditties about knowing where you're going. Parents warned about not getting lost. One wise person observed simply, "If you don't know where you're going, how will you know when you get there?" In the world of management, it was put most succinctly by Charles Hughes, then of Texas Instruments, when he observed tersely, "We can know whether what we are doing is absurd only after we have determined the goals we seek to achieve." According to management polls, fewer than one manager in ten asks what is the most important goal for the day. If you don't know the most important goal for the day, can you know the most important actions to be taken? You can't!

Failure to Set Objectives

The cost of not setting objectives is clear. When the goal or direction is uncertain, it is impossible to know whether what you are doing is effective, or a waste of time—whether a given decision is *right* or *useless*. When the objective hasn't been set, you can't know when you've achieved it, and you can't *measure progress* along the way. What you *can* know is that if you arrive at somewhere worthwhile, it has been by chance rather than good management!

When our priorities are not clear, we don't know where to put our main emphasis or concentrate our efforts, and we wonder why at the end of the day we feel at loose ends. Furthermore, when we don't have priorities of our own, we say yes to too many requests of others, whether important or not. We are continually interrupted—we drift from one task to another, leaving many of them unfinished. When we don't impose deadlines on ourselves, we may never get around to the *real* priority for the day—because we *never* have time to get *everything* done. And if we fail to check our progress on key tasks, we can find ourselves running out of time and in the middle of another crisis.

Why We Don't Plan

"I don't have *time* to plan" is the common complaint heard from many women. You may agree that planning is important, while protesting your ability to accomplish it in view of the overburdening tasks you face. It's a dilemma faced by many women and men. For example, the amazing results of a survey of 500 chief executives showed that 83 percent of those responding didn't have time to read to keep up with their field, and 72 percent (an astonishing three-fourths!) did not have time to think or plan. If these were chief executives, and three-fourths of them weren't thinking or planning, one must query what *were* they doing? Whatever it was surely was not as important as thinking and planning— the most difficult, yet most important work of not only executives, but all of us.

One flimsy excuse for not planning is that to plan is to limit your options. Some people feel that a plan locks them into a set pattern of activities which limits their freedom to respond to opportunities. What a good plan *does* do is map the best course of action to achieve your predetermined objectives. What better course to be "locked into"? And who says that the best-laid plan cannot be changed if unforeseen opportunities arise?

Day-to-Day Crises Take Over

A common barrier to planning is the emphasis on day-to-day operations which comes most naturally to you as a manager, whether in your office or your home. When problems arise, you want to be involved in solving them. No one minds sharing the credit for solving a problem. If it's a crisis, all the more reason for getting involved. It feels good to be a heroine! (Some crises are allowed to happen for this very reason.) Furthermore, involvement in day-to-day problems can give you instant gratification. Long-range planning, on the other hand, seems not only filled with uncertainty, but also demands the deferment of satisfactions. Also, immediate problems have an urgency which makes them hard to ignore. Just as the rewards for solving them will be immediate, so will be the penalties for ignoring them. So planning is neglected, which means that even more problems will arise, necessitating even more firefighting and crisis management.

Where Do I Start?

"Tomorrow," lamented the harried office supervisor, "I've just *got* to get organized." This manager was stating a common frustration. The job had gotten on top of her. She was sinking into a sea of paperwork, memos, and trivia on her desk. One such manager attended a time management seminar. At coffee break she commented to one of the authors that if this seminar didn't solve her problem, she was resigning from her profession. Her job had gotten to be too much for her, and she now could hardly face going in to work. Her cluttered desk was a mute accusation that she couldn't handle it—couldn't even get organized!

Winston Churchill may have suggested why getting organized and setting goals is one of the most difficult tasks for all of us when he observed, "It is difficult to look into the future further than you can see." The shape of the future does depend on many forces difficult to foresee, and the further you look into it, the more uncertain it becomes.

In addition to the uncertainty, there is the fear of being evaluated or held accountable. Who willingly sets goals against which she will be measured, and risks failure? Especially if it isn't asked for or somehow can be avoided? The risk of failure is one of the greatest difficulties in getting people to set goals.

When that resistance is overcome, and people do set goals, another big difficulty is in making sure that the goals are realistic and achievable yet are not *too* easy. A cautious team member might understate goals to ensure success. When you face the problem of a subordinate deliberately understating goals, you need skill, patience, and firmness to handle the situation effectively.

Criteria of Effective Goals

If goal-setting is important, how can you increase the chances of your goals being reached successfully? There are specific criteria you can follow. For example, effective goals should be:

Specific and measurable, so that you will know when you have achieved them. To say, "My goal is to delegate more" is not specific enough. "More" can mean anything you want it to mean. If you delegate the sharpening of pencils to your secretary, you could say you had delegated more—yet that would be meaningless in comparison with the delegation of major tasks.

Attainable, to prevent frustration. Nothing is more discouraging than to face too many tasks for the time available, or tasks that are too difficult for the ability or resources you bring to the job.

Worthwhile, in order to motivate, to achieve, or be *worth* working for. Robert Browning said that one's *reach* should exceed one's *grasp*. If goals require stretch they will be rewarding when achieved.

Consistent with those of your boss, organization, or committee. They should be supportive of the overall direction of the team effort.

Written, and reviewed occasionally so they won't be forgotten. You cannot do what you can't remember!

Participative, to ensure commitment. Imposed goals may be accepted, but will not receive the same underlying commitment as when those responsible for achieving them have participated in setting them. No one wants to see her *own* goals fail.

Deadlined to ensure that they will be taken seriously. Everyone faces so many deadlines that it is difficult to take anything seriously without one. You think to yourself that you'll do it when you get around to it. Well, "getting around to it" is rarely as simple as it sounds. Deadlines help us get around to those things that need doing.

Flexible, in case conditions change over which you have no control. Goals should not be changed simply to meet performance. However, when situations beyond your control change dramatically and make predetermined goals *unattainable*, then goals should be reexamined in fairness to the one responsible for achieving them.

After Goals Come Priorities

After goals are determined, priorities need to be set. It is possible to have clearly defined goals but *not* have meaningful priorities because you've not ranked the goals in order of importance.

Priorities are given surprisingly little attention by many of us. How to set them, how to distinguish between different kinds, how to stick to them, how to resolve conflicting priorities—these are skills that many of us have left undeveloped.

Criteria for Setting Priorities

How does one set priorities? By applying a set of criteria:

1. long-range importance,
2. short-range urgency, and
3. growth trend

Ask yourself how important a particular goal is to your overall plans for the organization or department or home. Then ask whether it has a short-range urgency or a long-range importance. Finally, if it is a problem, has it peaked? What is its growth trend? If it will go away if left alone, leave it alone. However, if the problem is growing and is clearly a potential crisis if left unattended, give it a higher relative priority.

STICKING TO THE PRIORITIES.   Setting priorities may be one thing. Sticking to them is quite another. *Persistence in pursuing priorities* may be the most overlooked tool in effective management. The trick in sticking to priorities is *not to tolerate interruptions* (except, of course, in case of real emergencies). A whole host of interruptions continually vie for attention. We shall see in Chapter 9 what steps should be taken to control them.

CONCENTRATE ON THE CRITICAL MATTERS.   Experts have used the Pareto Principle to demonstrate that effective time managers concentrate on the few critical actions which will bring the greatest results. Vilfredo Pareto, an Italian economist, observed that 80 percent of his country's wealth was concentrated in the hands of 20 percent of the people. The same relative ratio between *actions* and *results* has been observed in a wide variety of human endeavors. Most of the complaints in any organization will come from a relatively small number of its personnel. The bulk of sales volume in most organizations will be accounted for by relatively few customers. Out of these observations came the conclusion that "the *significant* items in a given group normally constitute a relatively small portion of the total items in the group." This is the Pareto Principle.

Reflection convinces most people that indeed, the most effective people they know seem not to waste time on trivia; they focus their efforts on worthwhile, important, strategic matters. They manage somehow to ignore or delegate the less important things. Since there is never time to get *every- thing* done, what a clever way to ensure that what *doesn't* get done are the less important matters!

THE CHARLES SCHWAB EXPERIENCE. Charles Schwab, when he was president of Bethlehem Steel, learned an un- forgettable lesson about the Pareto Principle and the utility of planning the day's work around it. Dissatisfied with his ability to get as much done as he would like, he confronted a friend and consultant, Ivy Lee, with this unusual challenge: "Show me a way to get more things done with my time," he said, "and I'll pay you any fee within reason." Handing Schwab a sheet of paper, Lee said, "Write down the most important tasks you have to do tomorrow and number them in order of importance. When you arrive in the morning, begin on No. 1 and stay on it till it's completed. Recheck your priorities, then start on No. 2. If any task takes all day, never mind, so long as it's still No. 1. If you don't finish them all you probably couldn't with any other method either, and without any system you're likely not even to have decided what was most important. Make this a habit every working day. When it works for you give it to your people. Try it as long as you like. Then send me your check for what you think it's worth."

Some weeks later Schwab sent Lee a check for $25,000, with a note saying that the lesson was the most profitable he had ever learned. In five years this plan was, according to Charles Schwab, largely responsible for turning Bethlehem Steel Corporation into the largest independent steel pro- ducer in the world. When queried by friends about paying so large a fee for so simple an idea, Schwab responded by asking what ideas were not basically simple. He reminded them that for the first time not only he but his entire team was getting first things done first. On reflection he stated that perhaps the expenditure had been the most valuable investment Bethlehem Steel had made all year.

What to Plan First—Short Range, or Long?

Curiously, the best approach to planning and organizing the *day* is in recognizing that this is *not* where to start. It is impractical to plan what must be done today if we have no clear idea of what must be done this week. And that isn't possible if the goals for the month aren't clear. Those goals can't be clear if there are no annual objectives. *So planning starts long-range, then moves short-range*. When a target for the year has been agreed upon, a time line is drawn from that target date back to the present, as shown in Figure 1. Thus target dates for the month and week are automatically set, or at least approximated.

Figure 1

TIME LINE FOR ANNUAL OBJECTIVE—PROJECT X

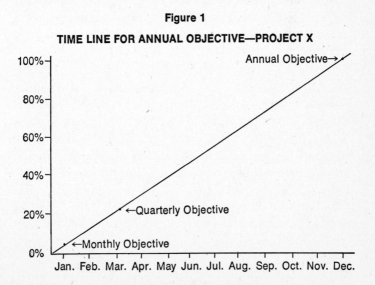

Developing a Time Line

TIME FRAMES FOR PLANNING.   The four most common
time frames for planning are the year, the month or quarter,
the week, and the day. When E. B. Osborn said that after
planning and organizing the day, all else in the life of a
manager was but child's play, there were those who took
exception. Doesn't everyone know that the further ahead
one plans the more uncertain and therefore the more difficult
it becomes? How can deciding what to do today compare
in any way with the complexities of planning for a whole
year?

Osborn undoubtedly was referring to the relative ease
with which a target can be set when there will be plenty of
time to review it as the year progresses. He also may have
observed the struggle of the typical person in determining
what the first step should be and *finding a way to make
it happen*. Indeed, *making it happen* is the final test for any of
us. As we've already seen, everything seems to get in the
way of making it happen. Nothing gets done by itself, and
before we get around to making the right things happen, a
host of paperwork, crises, calls, visits, memos, and inciden-
tals cry out for attention. The unwary woman succumbs,
and the critical tasks are postponed for that never-to-arrive
day "when I get around to it."

ANNUAL OBJECTIVES.   A standard three-ring notebook
makes an ideal "desk workbook." One section should be
entitled "Annual Objectives" and might well include at the
front a list of the eight criteria for sound objectives. (See
page 49.) In Figure 2 a simple chart is shown for listing one's annual objectives or goals. The purpose of this and
the following charts is simply to track or follow a long-range
objective (Project X) from inception to the day of completion.

Figure 2

ANNUAL OBJECTIVES

Prior-ity	A. Annual Goals	19— year	Due Date To be done in month of	Follow-up Dates			
	1. Project X 2. 3. 4. 5.		April 15	1/15	2/15	3/15	

MONTHLY GOALS. Figure 3 shows a chart for listing monthly goals. Note in the example shown that Project X is entered, since this is the month for completion of that project as shown in the preceding annual goals chart (Figure 2).

A section in your desk notebook should include tabs or sections for "Monthly Goals" with at least twelve tabs for the entire year. As one month is completed, it is recommended that a new month be added, so that twelve future months are in the plans at all times.

WEEKLY GOALS. In Figure 4 a weekly plan sheet is shown; it is similar to the one designed by E. B. Osborn for use by the managers in his organization. Note that Project X is recorded under "Projects," since this is the week indi-

Figure 3

Prior-ity	B. Monthly Goals	April month	Due Date To be done in week of	Follow-up Dates			
	1. Project X 2. 3. 4. 5.		April 15	4/1	4/8		

Figure 4

WEEKLY PLAN SHEET

Week of ___. *April 15*___

Prior-ity	Phone	Meetings
1	*BH re: Project X Promotion*	

	Write	Appointments

	Projects	Lunches
1	*Project X Completion*	

cated in the monthly chart (Figure 3) for completion of this project.

DAILY PLAN.   Figure 5 shows the daily plan with Project X listed, since this is the day indicated in the weekly

Figure 5

WRITTEN DAILY PLAN

Date _____ *April 15* _____

Prior-ity	Objectives	Deadline
1	*Project X*	*11:00*
2	*Pricing Review*	*12:00*
3	*Annual Sales Plan*	*3:30*
4		
5		

plan sheet (Figure 4) for completion of this project. Note that deadlines are indicated for each of the major tasks for the day. This not only provides you with the incentive for completing tasks in an orderly manner without spending more time on them than is warranted, but is also an excellent reason for saying no to interruptions which may be less important than the project you're working on. You now have the option of saying "Sorry, Betty, I've got a ten o'clock deadline for this. Could I call you back later, or do you suppose John could help you with it?"

Realistic Goals for Office and Home

Let's examine some specific goals or objectives in terms of the criteria suggested earlier. Two examples of work-related goals are: (1) to plan the launch of a particular project (Project C) in six months' time, and (2) to plan to develop and implement a performance evaluation program (Program D) within one year. The two goals suggested as examples for home are: (1) to plan to complete the redecorating of the home in six months, and (2) to plan for next year's vacation.

A glance at the eight criteria suggests that these goals meet those requirements. They are specific, measurable, attainable, and worthwhile; their consistency with other goals of your organization or home can easily be assessed. If they are in writing they will be much more likely to be remembered and pursued successfully.

Let's assume, for the sake of analysis, that these goals were *not* arrived at participatively. The two goals at work were your own decision and you had not discussed them with your team or associates. When you do so, they may be surprised and object because they have other commitments they consider more important. You are now embroiled in the most difficult of problems: that of resolving priorities in conflict, with the almost certain result that regardless of what is agreed upon, morale will suffer.

As far as goals for the home, where living and leisure are so intimately interwoven, any major project which will affect the lives of all is a tremendous opportunity for building team work and esprit de corps—and conversely, any major project which is unilaterally imposed risks less than wholehearted compliance and even downright resistance. Planning remodeling, decorating, gardening, and vacations, for example, can be positive and rewarding experiences or can be exercises in futility.

Note that the goals are also deadlined. Dates can always be adjusted if necessary. If adjustments are needed, the sooner, the better—since the later a problem is discovered, the more difficult the change may be, and the more likely it is to cause difficulties to others involved.

Set Your Own Goals

In the space provided in Figure 6 write two goals or objectives, one for your work and one for your home. As you think about each, measure it against the eight criteria for good goal-setting. Make sure each is specific and measurable, attainable, worthwhile, consistent, written, participative (if appropriate), and deadlined.

Figure 6

YOUR GOALS

Completion Date

Goal for work: _____   _____

_____   _____

Goal for home: _____   _____

_____   _____

Criteria for goals: Place a check mark in the appropriate space to indicate that each goal satisfies the eight criteria for sound objectives. If a criterion is not applicable at this time, indicate with "N/A." For example, the criterion of "flexible" for certain goals may be difficult to determine at the outset. If a certain criterion is not met, determine how the goal can be revised or what action to take to meet it. For example, if it was not arrived at participatively, can discussion be initiated with your team as a way to provide meaningful participation?

	Goal for Work	Goal for Home
1. Specific and measurable	_____	_____
2. Attainable	_____	_____
3. Worthwhile	_____	_____
4. Consistent	_____	_____
5. Written	_____	_____
6. Participative	_____	_____
7. Deadlined*	_____	_____
8. Flexible	_____	_____

     * Are most of the home deadlines automatic?

In a very real sense, choosing goals and planning to achieve them is where it all begins in managing your time. It is the rational predetermination of where you want to go and how you intend to get there. Until this has been done you can never be sure that your time is being well spent. As the Roman philosopher Seneca admonished, "For the ship without a harbor, no wind is the right one." So it is for you. Without a goal and plans to achieve it, your decisions are left to chance. No woman would choose to leave her time and her life to chance!

6

MANAGING
CRISIS SITUATIONS

. . . to have a crisis and act upon it is one thing. To dwell in perpetual crisis is another.

<small>BARBARA GRIZZUTI HARRISON (1975)</small>

So common are crises that many women have signs posted in their homes or offices depicting the humor of such incidents. Two such signs have achieved international notoriety. The first goes back at least to World War II: "If you can keep your head in all this confusion, you just don't understand the situation." The second, of more recent but equally anonymous origin, reads: "I'm going to have a nervous breakdown! I've worked for it . . . I've earned it . . . and nobody is going to deprive me of it!"

Management by crisis ranks second on the worldwide list of timewasters, while lack of objectives, priorities, and planning ranks third. This isn't surprising, since the two timewasters often accompany each other and are positioned near the top of the timewaster profiles of most organizations. They appear to have a reciprocal effect on each other. For example, by failing to plan you are practically ensuring future crises. Conversely, when your day is consumed with "firefighting" and dealing with crises, you have no time to plan. As the popular saying goes, "When you're up to your neck in alligators, who cares that your objective was to drain the swamp?"

"Crisis" Defined

Winston Churchill, noted for his pithy remarks, made a provocative comment about crisis management. He took a nap each day. His instructions were: "I will be awakened only in the event of a crisis. I further define 'crisis' to mean the armed invasion of the British Isles."

The term *crisis* has been used so often in so many ways that we need to define what we mean by it. In the context of this book we define crisis to mean an unexpected interruption, of major impact, from the normal course of events, necessitating immediate response. We define crisis management to mean reacting to problems as they occur, rather than anticipating them and taking steps to prevent them or to limit their consequence. Although crisis management ranks second among all timewasters worldwide, very few persons have ever stopped to ask why it happens or how to prevent its recurrence.

The Causes of Crises

The painful cost of constantly recurring crises scarcely needs reciting. You know that under such pressure you act in haste without the benefit of deliberation, without the opportunity of exploring better alternative courses. The phrase

"The hurrieder I go, the behinder I get" describes the trap of being tyrannized by the urgent instead of focusing on the really important matters which ought to be getting your attention.

Murphy's three laws apply to crisis management, and they should be taken seriously. The first, *Nothing is as simple as it seems,* suggests that we tend to underestimate the difficulty of the tasks we face. This leads to the second law: *Everything takes longer than you think.* By underestimating the difficulty of tasks we will also underestimate the time required to complete them. Therefore deadlines will be unrealistic. What happens next is capsulized in the third law: *If anything CAN go wrong, it WILL.* We should call Murphy's laws "the chronology of a crisis," since they sum up so much of what goes wrong in our crisis-filled lives.

Of course there are other causes of crises. Primary among them are the lack of sound planning and the failure to monitor progress in time to take corrective action. How many times do we discover *too late* that a critical deadline will not be met! We tend to blame others when, in fact, the fault is more likely our own for not anticipating the problem and taking steps to prevent it.

Indeed, the failure to anticipate problems is almost certainly the number-one cause of crises. Note that it is included as a factor in the very definition of crisis management. Human nature seems to dictate that once a plan is made everyone assumes that everything will be done according to plan and that nothing will happen to derail it. As we noted, Murphy's third law holds to the contrary—that if anything *can* go wrong, it *will*! You know what a "bad day" can be like: Your best-laid plans have gone awry! Although you'd planned the dinner party well in advance, made lists, enlisted your husband's support, and arranged for the children's care, when the day of the party arrives . . . the disposal stops working, the baby-sitter calls and cancels, your husband has an unexpected work commitment to attend to, and you can't find the eighth napkin which goes with your favorite tablecloth. If anything *can* go wrong, it *will*!

While we fail to anticipate problems, we also fail to check up to see that things are going well, or to require progress reports so that we won't have to check up. After the failure of the American attempt to rescue the hostages in Iran, can you imagine the soul-searching of the planners in the Pentagon and White House? They must have queried, "What if we had *fully* anticipated the potential toll of sandstorms and mechanical failures, how many extra helicopters *should* we have ordered?"

Doing things we like, while putting off unpleasant tasks, has caused many crises. The all-too-human tendency to *procrastinate* may be the second greatest cause of crises. It's natural to postpone taking action in situations of uncertainty or high risk. But the action of postponement itself may be hazardous, especially when timing is critical.

In the work setting, a constant switching of priorities by the boss or top management often creates crises at lower levels and will ultimately destroy the morale of those who are "never permitted to finish a task without being interrupted for some new urgent order." Or need we mention the crises caused by members of a household who switch priorities but neglect to advise others who will be affected? Information blockages, inaccurate data, mechanical breakdown, and human error round out a long list of potential causes of this critical and costly timewaster, crisis management.

Solutions

Avoiding crisis management requires thought and disciplined action. Consider the obvious solutions. When your goal or objective is clear, *schedule the tasks* necessary to attain it. *Be sure the deadlines are realistic. Build in a cushion.* If you need the material by the fourteenth to meet your deadline, give the supplier a deadline of the tenth. *Get progress reports*. Check up on the eighth to see that the material will be forthcoming. Measure your own progress at regular intervals to ensure that problems will be discovered in time to correct them. Have a *contingency plan* for the crises most likely to result in the greatest damage to your project. List steps to limit them if they do occur.

Fast detection and *response* are two critical points. The DEW-line installation of sensitive radar networks on the far north Canadian and Alaskan borders is an "early warning system" designed to detect any incoming missiles or planes in time to alert our defense forces for effective counter measures. Avoid *overreacting*. It doesn't take much skill, as one sage put it, to massage a problem into a crisis. Most of us have done it wittingly or unwittingly on more than one occasion. Ignore the transitory problem. If it will go away, leave it alone. If someone else can handle it, delegate. React only to the degree warranted by the severity of the problem. Limit your response to avoid wasting time and effort, to avoid creating crises on the side, and to avoid being distracted from other major and more important pursuits.

You can begin immediately to avoid crisis management. As Valerie Jeglum, a data processing officer in a Washington state bank, says, "I get a lift I did not imagine possible from knowing that I have time to do those things I felt were important, but had not convinced myself that I had the right to place before the day-to-day crises. I'm a long way from my ideal, but I've got a foot on the path and it feels like this time I am going to be able to exert the self-discipline to stay on it."

Preventing Crises at Home

In your home steps can be taken in anticipation of crises. The police and fire department numbers should be clearly visible near or on the telephone. Fire extinguishers should be in handy locations and everyone versed in their use. Parents know that crises increase directly with the number of small children in the home. So potential hazards like scissors and sharp knives are kept out of reach. Smoke detectors and burglar alarms are crisis-preventing instruments to give early warning of fire or burglary. It is likely that women managers who have raised small children have an advantage over men in terms of experience and background for the management of crisis situations.

An excellent case in point would be Jerrie Hurd, who decided to write about her discovery that living at a crisis level at home was unnecessary.[1] A self-described middle-American housewife and mother of two, she recounted the day her husband arrived home at 5:00 P.M. to find her exhausted with dirty dishes in the sink, no supper started, and the baby crying. Her husband quoted some management expert who had stated that many businesses spend 80 to 90 percent of their time doing things which bring in only 10 to 20 percent of the profit (an application of the Pareto Principle).

Since "supper won't wait for profound thoughts," she waited till the next morning to assess her situation. She wondered whether she might be spending up to 90 percent of *her* time achieving only 10 percent of her rewards. Writing down her activities brought two swift conclusions: first, she was living at a crisis level, and second, she was spending an inordinate amount of her time doing things she did not enjoy. Her crisis living resulted primarily from her failure to anticipate tasks. She washed when the kids no longer had clean clothes. Then she had to wash whether or not it was convenient, which frequently it was not. While some tasks

[1] Jerrie W. Hurd, "Ceasefire on Crisis Living," *The Ensign,* August 1976.

couldn't be predicted or deferred when they occurred, such as changing the baby's diapers, most could be organized to provide better use of her time. Having a neat, uncluttered house was a pleasure, but not worth spending 90 percent of her waking hours to maintain. She decided it was not worth ironing permanent press even if it did look better that way. She organized her shopping to buy in larger quantities so she could make fewer trips. Low-value and distasteful tasks were eliminated or cut back, which made time for more important and more enjoyable things she'd always wanted to do. She refers to the irrefutable law that housework will fill the available time and countered it by allocating limited time to get it done. What might not get done waits.

To her amazement the priority system has worked. She begins with number one and works her way down till she runs out of time. If she doesn't get to the ironing for a few days, it soon becomes a priority item and gets done. Occasionally she takes all day to catch up, but the overall time spent on things that have to be done but have low value has decreased dramatically with no noticeable change in the quality of life her family enjoys. And she's a happier and more pleasant person to be around.

The definition of crisis management includes the crucial elements for its control: "Reacting to problems as they arise rather than *anticipating* them and taking steps to *prevent* them or to *limit* their consequence." Thus, the three critical steps are *anticipate, prevent,* and *limit.* We know that chance favors the prepared mind, so be prepared. Victor Hugo said: "Where no plan is laid, where the disposal of time is surrendered merely to chance, chaos soon reigns." You need not surrender your time and your life to chance, to chaos or to crisis management. The steps outlined in this chapter will enable you to control your time instead of letting it control you.

7

ORGANIZING YOUR OFFICE

Order is a lovely thing;
On disarray it lays its wing,
Teaching simplicity to sing.

ANNA HEMPSTEAD BRANCH (1910)

Organizing your office can be the key to your success! A slipshod job, not following through, and miscommunication are often the results of an inefficient or messy office. Lost documents, forgotten promises, and missed deadlines are common occurrences. Some women claim that the messier the office, the busier and more productive the occupant. (Doesn't some degree of disorganization go with creativity?) However, women discover that this notion is a myth when they actually organize their offices (and their homes!) for maximum efficiency. Good organization promotes both efficiency and effectiveness. Peter Drucker summed up efficiency as doing the job right; effectiveness as doing the *right* job right! With effectiveness comes increased productivity, enhanced satisfaction, less stress and anxiety, and more time for yourself.

A major contributor to a disorganized office is the occupant's lack of clarity about key result areas and also her specific job responsibilities. What *is* the scope of her activities? Several factors need to be considered: (1) the full range of her responsibilities; (2) her own ability as a planner, delegator, and controller; (3) the tasks of her subordinates, if any; (4) the experience and ability of her team; and (5) the physical layout.

The Functional Office: What Does It Look Like?

A well-organized office enables you to be more productive, *and* to get the job done faster. Setting aside a few hours or a day or two to undertake that organization will be well worth the time and effort.

Following basic rules makes a big difference. Supplies and equipment which are in greatest day-to-day demand need to be close to you. If you use a typewriter often during each day, have it immediately available where you can swing to it, or it to you—not where you have to walk to get to it.

A telephone holder allows you to talk comfortably on the phone while making notes without twisting your neck (or jamming your earring!). If you have a choice of touch systems for your phone, select the one which dials most quickly. There are phones which automatically redial busy numbers, while automatic dialing of preprogrammed numbers permits complete dialing with only the touch of a button. A speaker phone allows you to listen to the other person without having to pick up your own phone, or to be handling papers during the conversation.

Quality equipment and supplies are worth it! The typewriter that needs repair biweekly, the letterhead paper that not only looks flimsy but bleeds through, or the file cabinet that pulls hard or almost tips over each time it's opened do not equal efficiency or contribute to a positive mental attitude!

Physical comfort and aesthetic satisfaction are important considerations. How many times have you been depressed within seconds of walking into your office, either because of papers piled hither and yon reminding you of tasks undone or because the office itself is drab and dull? It's amazing what a cheery environment results when the walls are lightened, windows are washed, some inexpensive pictures or prints are hung, and attractive pillows and plants and perhaps a lamp are tastefully placed. Some hardy plants do very well in artificial light.

Physical comfort directly affects your creativity and productivity. Good lighting can prevent tired eyes and headaches, produce more alertness, a clearer head, and greater energy. Comfortable seating is a *must*. A desk chair which is adjustable in height and provides proper back support is the best insurance against pains in your back, legs, or feet.

What about your desk itself? A variety of options are possible so long as you end up with the best work arrangement for you. One option might be no desk at all! In some occupations, and a few specific jobs, a desk is not necessary, while a conference table and chairs might be. Choose what fits your needs best.

If a desk does make sense for you, be sure it meets your needs. Utilize the drawers to get your daily supplies as close as possible. Pens, pencils, staples, scissors, and paper should literally be no more than arm's length away. Invest in a *good* "organizer" for your desktop reference tools. If you often work with architectural plans or large printouts or

sheets of paper, an ideal arrangement might be one in which
the desk itself faces a wall, and your chair can swivel between it and a large table behind you. A conversational
grouping for less formal discussions is favored by many
managers when space permits.

The Cluttered Desk: All That Paper,
What Will I Do?

Is your desk always cluttered? Are papers strewn all over
your office—being misplaced, getting lost? As Stephanie
Winston suggests, "There are only three things that can be
done with a piece of paper: it can be thrown away, something can be done with it, or it can be temporarily put
away."[1]

One of the reasons we allow the papers to accumulate
on our desks is that we want to be sure not to forget anything. A German executive reported, "The things we want
to remember we put on top of our desk, where we will see
them. The problem is that it really works. Every time our
gaze wanders and we look at them, our train of thought is
broken. Then as the stacks grow higher, we are unable to
remember what's beneath the top, so we begin to look for
things in the stacks. Time is wasted both in retrieving lost
items and in the interruptions occasioned by looking at all
the items we didn't want to forget"[2]

Another reason why we hang on to all that paper is that
"I may need it sometime." In many cases, we even develop
an emotional attachment, whether it's a clipping about an
old friend, the first draft of a favorite project, or a memo
about another department's long-range planning process. A

[1] Stephanie Winston, *Getting Organized: The Easy Way to Put Your Life in Order* (New York: Norton, 1978).

[2] R. Alec Mackenzie, *The Time Trap* (New York: McGraw-Hill, 1975), p. 67.

good question to ask ourselves if we're hanging on to lots of paper is "If I do throw this away now and if I would have a need for it later, what other resources do I have to get a copy or at least enough of the information I would need—department files, friends, lawyer, yellow pages, and so on?" In most cases, there would be at least one resource available to retrieve either the identical information or a close fac-simile.

Specific steps to avoid desk clutter include the follow-ing: (1) For each session at your desk, set priorities. What items do you need to deal with and in what order? (2) Have on your desk only that item with which you're currently dealing. (3) Place the other items in either your desk or-ganizer or color-coded folders. (4) Stay with the current project until you've taken all possible action on it at this point in time. (5) After disposing of your initial project, re-check priorities and then move on to the next most impor-tant item. (6) If you have a secretary or aide, request that he or she place all items of interest to you in an "in basket" rather than scattering them on your desk. Also, if feasible, use that person as a resource in other ways to help you keep your desk clear.

The above suggestions may seem too restrictive to some. Certainly flexibility in these matters is advised. How-ever, even women who have previously thrived on clutter report that following some of these organizing techniques has helped them not only to get more done in less time, but also to feel better about their work and themselves.

A desk diary helps to keep you organized. Get one that is small enough to fit in either your purse or your briefcase. Any ideas or "things to do" that hit you while getting ready for bed, in the car, or shopping can be jotted down at a moment's notice. You can then dismiss that thought from your mind and only return to it later when you refer to your diary or notes. In addition, a daily record for planning future meetings, reports, and even social events—along with an accurate record of what has already transpired—will keep you in charge of your own schedule. Without such a note-keeping system, your attempt to carry around in your head all those ideas and "things to remember" not only clogs your brain but also results in the loss of excellent ideas— sometimes permanently.

Become a Wastebasket Expert!

Time management scholars believe that the art of wastebas-ketry is one of the most critical skills in managing one's work. Developing the intestinal fortitude to keep only those papers which are relevant and have a reasonable chance of being used in the future, and throwing the rest away, is a very important self-management tool. Cluttered desks and bulging files are costly in time and space!

Keeping a big wastebasket close at hand, and developing the fine art of "putting-the-most-into-your-wastebasket," is suggested by Auren Uris. If you have a secretary or assistant, have him or her screen the papers coming to you so that you see only those that are necessary and relevant.

Handle Mail Expeditiously

How you handle your mail says a lot about you psychologically. A study by Chicago's Dartnell Institute for Business Research showed that a typical executive spends two to three hours per day reading and answering mail. This enormous investment in time approximates four months out of each year just to handle correspondence. Why?

People "hang on" to their correspondence for a variety of reasons: (1) not knowing how to delegate, (2) a lack of confidence in the person to whom handling the mail would be delegated, (3) curiosity and wanting to know as much as possible about what's going on, and (4) a lack of discipline in work habits. All are factors which can keep you from handling your mail more effectively.

Some simple how-to's can ease the correspondence load considerably. If you have a secretary, he or she at the end of each day can assemble any mail not requiring your immediate attention to be either taken home by you or dealt with first thing in the morning.

An important rule to remember: Reply as quickly as possible and keep the reponse as short as possible. The longer you delay, the more lengthy the response is likely to be. Nothing more is called for, and the recipient will appreciate the saving of his or her time. In informal situations, answering on the original letter saves time all around. Run a copy for your files, or make brief notes of the date and contents.

All correspondence does not have to be dealt with in the office. Whether you use a portable dictating device or write your own personal notes and drafts by hand, an amazing amount of such work can be done while traveling, waiting for appointments, or while having your hair done. By using this "in-between" time you will find yourself getting things done faster and leaving time for yourself in the end.

A highly successful woman who heads a multimillion dollar corporation, Mary Kay Cosmetics, views her system of handling the mail to be a major timesaver for her. Mary Kay Ash reports: "My secretary reads and sorts the mail for me. The most urgent things are put in red file folders, labeled 'For Your Answer,' 'Needs Your Prompt Attention,' and 'For Your Signature.' Less urgent papers are put in plain files labeled 'Miscellaneous,' 'Advertisements,' etc.

"I handle all correspondence only one time, finding the answer to the letter on top before going on to another one,

which keeps me from handling the same piece of paper a
half-dozen times and trying to make a decision."

Your Filing System—A Plus or a Pain?

"Oh, no—you're really going to talk about filing? I've tried,
and it's hopeless. There's no way I can have an organized
filing system!" Before you throw in the towel for good,
consider these options. First, you may not need to set up the
system yourself. If at all possible, delegate to another person
the responsibility of setting up the system. Then you review
the plan before it's put into effect. This way, you have the
opportunity to make input and yet you don't have to take
the time to start from scratch. Also, have that person prepare a simple chart or set of instructions which describes the
filing system so that in the event of his or her absence others
can use the files efficiently.

Remember that files are an ongoing tool and, to some
extent, are always being added to and refined. A common
error in setting up files is to make too many categories—to
the point where there seems to be a separate file for each
new sheet of paper! It's better to start out with fewer categories; then, if a particular file begins to fill up and more and
more time is needed to track down items in it, that folder can
be divided into additional categories. Let your filing system
grow naturally! And just as plants often need pruning, so do
your files. Every six months or every year, the files need to
be reviewed; obsolete papers should be discarded and additional categories added, if necessary.

How long do you keep something in the files? Estimates
vary, but many experts say that 80 to 95 percent of materials
placed in files is never needed, not even once. Current operations files need not be kept more than one year and should
be readily accessible, while legal documents and other pa-

pers that have more long-term value can be filed in a special section or in a different location.

To Dictate . . . or Not?

Why do we resist dictating machines? For many women, it is fear that they "can't work it right." A related factor may be the unwillingness to take time to learn how to use the equipment. Also, secretaries who are anxious to keep up their shorthand skills may object to machine dictation.

However, using a dictating machine is a real timesaver! A Daniel Howard survey shows that 40 percent of managers write letters and memos in longhand for their secretaries to type. When you consider the agonizingly slow pace of handwriting (twenty to thirty words per minute at best), compared with the speed of the spoken word (150 words a minute), the utility of dictating equipment becomes apparent. Moreover, a person can dictate into a machine twice as fast as a secretary can record those same words in shorthand. Therefore the dictating machine is far superior to both handwritten copy and personal dictation to a secretary.

A portable dictating machine or recorder can be used away from the office, while driving a car or traveling by plane. Alexandra Armstrong, a senior executive with a financial planning firm, reports that she carries a dictating machine with her at all times. "If out of town, I'll dictate and then mail back the tapes to my secretary. I even keep my dictating machine next to my bed." Your ideas can be recorded while they are fresh, and once recorded are on the tape and off your mind!

Memo-mania

Memo-itis has afflicted the whole corporate world. It is a very time-consuming process. Each memo requires several steps: thinking through the intended message, dictating it, typing it, transmitting it, reading it, and—finally—disposing of it.

Eric Webster suggests with a touch of humor that while there are valid reasons for memos, often they are written for the wrong ones, such as:

1. The memo to postpone work—a note saying you are going to act enables you to do nothing for a little longer with a clear conscience.

2. The memo to demonstrate efficiency (not effectiveness)—"Following my memo of the first of last month . . ." (The real message is "I know what it says; let's see if you can find your copy.")

3. The militant memo—a tough-worded statement like "John, this situation can no longer be tolerated. It must be dealt with immediately!" (Often sent by the mild-mannered or insecure manager who is afraid to take a stand in person.)

4. The accusative memo designed "for the record." It's a "your fault" approach: If the recipient does answer it (which will take hours), the sender can always contest the answer; and if the recipient doesn't answer, she has him "fixed" in the files!

5. The status-making memo. "From the desk of . . ." might be more tasteful if simply "From . . ." in dignified but attractive type and paper. Desks don't send memos!

6. The "see-how-hard-I'm-working" memo is penned by the insecure subordinate who wants to prove her worth by inundating the boss with paper. Of course, all the time required to write the memo subtracts from time she could be devoting to her work.

7. The "blind copy" memo in which a person writes

ostensibly for one audience but is actually addressing the unseen, unlisted recipients of the blind copy.[3]

While critical observers generally agree that memos should be used sparingly, they do serve a useful purpose on occasion: to remind, to clarify, to confirm, or to put something important in writing for the record. However, memos are *one-way communication*. To accomplish two-way communication it is faster, easier, and more effective to make a phone call or deal with an issue face-to-face in conference. Monitor your use of memos. Were any of those you wrote last month either unnecessary or overlong? Ongoing monitoring can ensure that you send memos only when effective time utilization dictates.

Improve Your Reading Habits

Some women estimate that 30 percent of their on-the-job time is spent reading. If so, they will spend almost one year out of the next three reading! Certainly some professional reading is necessary. However, most of us do more than necessary, and consequently have less time available to fulfill other responsibilities.

How can reading be most effectively done? There are payoffs in delegating to others some of your reading. You can circulate materials quickly to interested people, asking them for feedback. Not only is the feedback valuable to you, but it saves your time and keeps your key people informed.

A great timesaver is learning to speed-read. In addition to private speed-reading schools, many colleges and universities offer such courses. Busy women report that learning

[3] Eric Webster, "Memo Mania," *Management Review*, September 1967.

this skill has been invaluable in increasing their productivity and efficiency. No wonder, for the average speed-reader more than doubles her reading speed, and at the same time increases her rate of comprehension! If you spend a third of your work time reading, and double your speed, that would in itself save over an hour a day, while improving your comprehension!

Another timesaver is to become very selective in your reading habits. Ask yourself, "What are the chances that I'll ever need the information from this article or book?" and "If I should ever need the information, can I get it easily another way?" These questions will help you eliminate much unnecessary reading.

When you do choose to read a magazine or book, you can still save time. Scan the table of contents for a rough idea of the content, and then read only those sections in which you're really interested.

Newer Alternatives at the Office

Flextime: Proving Beneficial to Both Employees and Employers

The utilization of flexible working hours, first introduced in the sixties in West Germany, has brought such measurable benefits to corporate business in America that the trend toward flextime has recently been expanding at an impressive rate of growth per year. An option particularly attractive to many women, the objectives are improved working conditions for employees and improved productivity for employers.

As reported by Jourdan Houston, "flexible scheduling slices the day into two segments—mandatory hours, or core time, during which all employees must be present; and discretionary hours, or band time, which fall on either side of the core."[4] Employees can vary their working hours so long

[4] J. Houston, *Kiwanis Magazine*, March 1978.

as they are present during the core time and work at least the agreed number of hours during a week or month. "If the core time is 9:30 A.M. to noon and from 1:30 to 4 P.M., on a given day an employee might arrive as early as 7 A.M. or stay as late as 6:30 P.M." Usually the "balance" of time (positive or negative) is carried forward to the next period.

Obviously such a system requires some controls and, in the case of large companies, some kind of checking-in-and -out apparatus. J. Carroll Swart in *A Flexible Approach to Working Hours* lays out advantages and disadvantages of the flextime system and tells you how to go about starting one for your organization. The smaller the organization, the simpler the system can be; its advantages have been demonstrated even in offices with only three or four employees. Writing in the ITT magazine *Profile* for the summer 1977 issue, Gabor Weiner, a Hungarian-born, Belgium-based flextime expert, described systems that can be ordered or adapted for up to thousands of employees. Some management time is involved in getting it in operation, and if a large system is needed, of course the apparatus could be expensive. However, even the time spent in getting it organized can have good results, because people do have to be able to cover for one another, learn each other's jobs, and take on more responsibility. In times of illness or employees moving away, this can be a tremendous side benefit.

The American Management Association found in a survey that of 196 companies that had tried it, 92 percent adopted flextime permanently. One company found that a long-standing tardiness problem and clock-watching disappeared, employee turnover fell by 75 percent, and productivity jumped. Because the work day starts at arrival time, tardiness and absenteeism almost disappeared. Work erosion (slow starts and afternoon lethargy) lessened, and employers in the survey reported that their people became more efficient and worked faster.

Obviously, flexible hours are a tremendous boon to the working woman who is trying to juggle two jobs (home and office)—often complicated by the responsibility of caring for children. But enthusiastic boosters also include men who want more time with their families, for athletics or hobbies, to finish an assignment for a deadline, or to avoid wasting time in rush-hour traffic.

In the search for improving the work environment, flex-time (or "glidetime" as it is sometimes called) has become a popular concept. Most of its users are convinced that its benefits far outweigh any shortcomings.[5]

A Second Look at Open Office Landscaping

The merits of open office landscaping are now being questioned. When "open office landscaping" was first introduced, it was designed to enhance the working environment of lower-level supervisors and technicians who were working in open, undivided areas. By installing low, attractively designed, movable partitions, it was possible to provide relative privacy while enhancing the appearance of the surroundings.

Not surprisingly, this move met with instant success, as evidenced in one large company in Sweden. It was a huge room that once housed more than a hundred people without benefit of any separations. The relentless sound of typewriters and adding machines rang continuously throughout. After landscaping, the area appeared attractively separated into sound-suppressing areas. No two people appeared to be too closely situated. Everyone obviously was pleased with the increased privacy, reduced noise level, and attractive surroundings.

---

[5] For a copy of the U.S. Civil Service Commission's "Flextime Guide," send $1.00 to Superintendent of Documents, Government Printing Office, Washington, D.C., 20402. More than one copy, 65¢. Bulk rates on request.

Unfortunately, the instant success of the idea at the lower levels of management led to predictable promotion of the idea for higher management levels. Of course, the promotion emphasized other benefits, since senior managers already had private offices with doors which could be closed when they wished not to be interrupted. Since more of them could be compressed into smaller space and since movable partitions added an element of flexibility to a growing or changing organization, economics and flexibility became the principal claimed benefits.

What was *not* discussed by the promoters of the concept was what it did to managers who were required to give up their offices for what many referred to as "those five-sided cubicles." They were usually much smaller in size (economy), had low partitions which could be peered over by any tall person (air conditioning prevented high partitions), and, most surprisingly, had no doors (economy and easy access). The lack of doors, the managers were told, would enhance communication. Unfortunately, it did—but with the wrong result, since it enhanced drop-in visitors and socializing (two of the top timewasters of managers worldwide). In addition, telephone conversations could be overheard by anyone on the other side of the five partitions! Communication was indeed enhanced—but the wrong kind, the kind that needs to be controlled, not promoted.

The promoters said that there would be conference rooms provided for those who needed privacy. But the inadequate numbers of these rooms and the sheer inconvenience of having to move outweighed this supposed benefit. In fact, as many dispossessed managers have said, if as many conference rooms were provided as are often needed, there would have to be one per manager—and then the corporation would have been far ahead to leave the original office plan.

We have had three memorable experiences with the concept of open office landscaping. First there was the favorable experience in Sweden with lower-level super-visors. Second, there have been countless managers in seminars who have responded, almost universally, that they do not like it because it interferes drastically with their ability to concentrate without interruption and to operate with a degree of privacy when necessary.

Third, and perhaps most interesting of all, was a one-day time management seminar conducted for the management team of one of the world's largest producers of open office landscaping equipment. When this subject came up in the course of developing solutions to the timewasters of drop-in visitors and socializing, it became quickly apparent that the great majority of their managers agreed that traditional offices would be the answer.

The benefits of open office landscaping have been over-sold to the management community. It will benefit lower levels by adding to their privacy, but it *harms* the effectiveness of senior managers and demotivates them as well. If economy and flexibility are that important, as in the case of one of our state governments, then open office landscaping *may* be justified. But, if the ability of a management team to function effectively is a paramount concern, as it ought to be, then these apparent benefits may be much too costly in the long run. Many organizations which had installed open offices are changing back. One of them spent nearly three-quarters of a million dollars to put in the open landscaping—only to face a virtual revolution of their entire management team. They took it out.

If your organization is considering it, talk extensively with managers who have experienced it—and not just the financial people who may be preoccupied with savings. Then look around at the number of offices where filing cabinets have been moved to partially block open doorways, where boxes have been stacked up to heighten partitions, where desks have been turned away from open doors—and draw your own conclusions. These are all attempts to regain lost privacy. Think how difficult it would be to maintain a "quiet hour" in full view of everyone coming to your door—even if your secretary or assistant *is* trying to head off interruptions.

In addition, some managers or group leaders, as well as engineers, architects, and designers, require wall and/or table space to lay out large charts or drawings. All of these factors must be taken into account by employers as they consider any kind of office redesign or renovation.

Whether a secretary, personnel manager, or executive, we all have a psychological need for a certain level of privacy, and to have adequate space and equipment to fulfill the requirements of our specific jobs with the least stress possible. The private office, with a door which can be opened or closed at will, clearly seems the choice of those who recognize that human resources are our most important asset, and that management time and morale merit the same effort at conservation as our budgets.

8

DELEGATION . . .
THE NAME
OF THE GAME

. . . to get caught up, and stay caught up, by working
through others. Delegation is the usual word for it.
The backbone of modern business, it is also helpful
in small business and for individuals.

DONALD AND ELEANOR LAIRD[1]

Ask yourself what the following three situations have in
common:

    1. A team member asks you what you think she ought
to do about a certain problem. After offering your opinion,
you recall discussing a similar problem with her a short time
ago and giving her essentially the same opinion then.

[1] Donald A. and Eleanor C. Laird, *The Techniques of Delegating*
(New York: McGraw-Hill, 1957).

2. Recognizing that a task you have just assigned a person is of special interest to your boss, and fearing that it may not be done perfectly, you tell the subordinate to check with you before making a critical move on it.

3. You've decided to start having phone calls and drop-in visitors screened by your very effective secretary. Because of her experience you realize she can do this without offending anyone. To save time and to gain the benefits immediately, you tell her to begin the practice at once; you further stipulate that if anyone seems surprised or unhappy about it, you will explain the reasons to them.

Although these three instances seem totally unrelated, they do have a common thread. Each represents a failure of delegation.

In the *first* case you are falling victim to reverse delegation. Since you have gone through a similar conversation and given your subordinate a similar opinion earlier, it is time that this subordinate stop coming to you for answers. It could well be your fault for encouraging overdependence by always coming up with answers instead of asking the questioner what *she* thinks ought to be done, and reminding her of the previous discussion.

In the *second* case you have the typical problem of overcontrol. After assigning the task you should leave the method of execution to the other person (who may well discover a better method than yours). To require a subordinate to check with you before making any critical moves is to remove the authority to take action on her own, thus violating the principle of "commensurate authority" (authority must be proportional to responsibility for optimum results).

In the *third* case you are involved in a more subtle form of delegating responsibility without authority. It appears evident that the practice of screening will not be expected by everyone, and therefore some callers or visitors may be sur-

prised and offended. In effect, the authority of the secretary
to screen them will be in question. This authority should
not be left in doubt, and would not be if you notified important clients and co-workers of the practice *in advance*. It
would then be clear that your secretary was doing this because you asked her to. It would be on your authority, not
her own.

These three common cases are only a sampling of the
many diverse aspects of delegation. It is surely one of the
most critical, most complicated, and least understood of all
timesaving activities. Consider for a moment that the very
definition of management assumes skill in delegation. If we
define management as "achieving objectives *through others*," it is clear that failure in delegation means failure in
managing. You can't get things done through others if you
can't delegate.

Benefits of Delegation

To appreciate that delegation is one of the most critical of all
timesaving activities, one need only review its benefits:

1. Leverages effectiveness by extending what one can *do*
   to what one can *get done* through others.
2. Releases time for more important work.
3. Maintains decision making at the lowest possible level
   where the required information and judgment exist.
4. Develops subordinates' initiative, skills, knowledge,
   competence, and job satisfaction.

It is doubtful that any other leadership function or activity can approach the benefits to the practitioner summarized
above. A personal testimonial to the value of improved delegation skills is given by Mona Carmack, Director of the
Public Library in Ames, Iowa. She states: "I have learned
delegation so well that after returning from several days out

of town, my desk might have one note of an informational nature, and a very few items of mail placed on it.'' With a touch of humor she adds, ''I have to wear a name tag so that my staff knows I'm still the director!''

Yet, if the benefits are so great, why is successful delegation so rare? The answer doubtless lies in a complex variety of reasons.

Reasons for Ineffective Delegation

Insecurity and fear of failure, coupled with lack of confidence in others, prevent many women from delegating. Curiously, this phenomenon occurs even with people whose skills and abilities are not equal to those of some subordinate who could have been delegated the task. Women often seem convinced that if they do something themselves it will be done right and they will know that it has been done right. You don't have to worry about whether someone else did it wrong or less effectively than you would have liked, or perhaps got it done too late. This ''do-it-yourself'' syndrome is something we're all guilty of at times. It may be a particular weakness for women whose role in the home happens to be the one in which you often do things yourself to save the hassle of getting someone else to do it.

Feeling more comfortable ''doing'' than ''managing'' is another common cause of failure to delegate. Clearly it is one to which women managers are prone because of their relative lack of experience in management roles. Also, the prevalent self-image women have had through the centuries defines them as the ones who carry out the directives or ideas of men, not those who give the directives themselves.

Ability and competence coupled with ego and a need to achieve may also play an important role in failure to delegate. Everyone wants to do well, and we all naturally gravitate to the things we do well. A ''be perfect'' approach may easily result in standards which virtually require that tasks be performed by ourselves, since no one else can measure up to our excessively high level of expectation.

Inability to establish appropriate checkpoints makes many women fearful that they will lose control if they delegate. This is a haunting fear, especially when combined with fear of failure and lack of confidence in staff. It virtually immobilizes many women when it comes to assigning work to others.

Failure to follow up—to provide for regular progress reports at predetermined intervals—means that many tasks which have been delegated will be executed poorly and the mistakes not discovered in time to take corrective action. Conversely, overcontrol or excessively detailed follow-up will destroy motivation of subordinates to perform delegated tasks well.

The failure to delegate authority to others that is appropriate to the responsibility delegated is one of the most common, but least identified, causes of failure in delegation. The secretary who is asked to screen calls for the boss who has failed to inform others of her intention is but one of dozens of examples. Responsibility was assigned, but the necessary authority to carry it out was lacking because the boss failed to tell others what to expect.

One of the most interesting of all delegation failures occurs when upward or reverse delegation is encouraged unwittingly by leaders. The person in charge often expects her subordinates to bring all their questions to her. If this practice is continued for too long or practiced excessively, an attitude of overdependence results in which subordinates are afraid to make decisions on their own, or find it too convenient to bring their problems to that leader. Even opinions expressed to subordinates may be taken as decisions, or at least have that effect if they unduly influence the decisions of those subordinates.

One of the most difficult delegation problems to solve is the top person in the organization who expects those next in line "to know all the details." Autocratic "bosses" are known for this demanding and unreasonable expectation. If you are expected to have all the answers whenever asked, you can hardly risk delegating anything. A parallel mistake of such bosses is to demand that subordinates answer their own phones, rather than having their calls screened (as most effective managers do) by a competent secretary or assistant.

When you are understaffed for a given workload or when your associates are inadequate or untrained, your delegation will obviously suffer.

Uncertainty over tasks and inability to explain rank high among causes of ineffective delegation. Either would cause a leader to hesitate before delegating. Misunderstandings resulting from poor instruction and the failure to request feedback have been responsible for many ill-performed tasks which were originally delegated with every expectation that they would be well performed.

A rare cause of failure to delegate, but one which could particularly affect women, is the fear of developing or bringing too much credit to a subordinate who is already threatening to overshadow you. For example, because of the relatively few women who have been promoted into higher levels of management and because of some being promoted above their ability level, those women have often felt unusually threatened by others working for them. As a result of feeling threatened, the female executives have sometimes not delegated or encouraged their subordinates.

Another factor impeding successful delegation is the inability of disorganized subordinates to delegate their overload of work, which in turn means that they cannot accept more responsibility. A person already working twelve to fourteen hours a day is hardly a prime prospect for additional delegated responsibility. This often occurs in volunteer service agencies in which both staff members and volunteers are overloaded with responsibility, resulting in less effectiveness because of lowered morale, attempting too much at once, and crisis management.

A review of the above causes of ineffective delegation should convince the most skeptical that delegation is indeed one of the most critical, most complex, and least understood of all managerial functions. When Charles Percy, the well-known U.S. Senator, assumed the presidency of Bell & Howell prior to his election to the Senate, he became a victim of failure to delegate. As he later related to Joseph Cooper, "I was so busy doing things I should have delegated that I didn't have time to manage."[2]

Steps to Successful Delegation

So essential is delegation to effective management, whether at home or in the office, that it is not surprising to find that the steps to successful delegating mirror those of effective management. Briefly summarized, they are:

1. *Clarify and prioritize your goals*, to ensure optimum direction of effort.
2. *Decide which of these goals others can handle*, to conserve your own time for top-priority tasks which only you can handle.
3. *Select the best persons*, matching task demands with their individual capabilities.
4. *Organize tasks for delegation*, to promote coordination and execution.
5. *Give clear instructions and request feedback*, to ensure understanding and motivation

[2] Joseph Cooper, *How to Get More Done in Less Time*, rev. ed. (Garden City: Doubleday, 1971).

6. *Set deadlines and provide for regular progress reports*, to ensure timely corrective action if needed.

In Chapter 5 we discussed the need for clear goals and priorities, without which directed effort is impossible. The net effect of lack of such direction is wasted time and effort. Another effect is uncertainty about what is really important to accomplish and therefore what to delegate. Note that delegation involves practically all of the managerial functions. Not only are clear *goals* and *plans* necessary before a decision on what to delegate can be made, but tasks to be delegated must be *organized*, which may involve personnel, equipment, facilities, and finances. Then appropriate persons must be selected to whom to delegate (*staffing*), and the actual *delegation* executed with well-*communicated* instructions. *Controls* in the form of progress reports at predetermined intervals must be provided, and in each of the above steps rational *decisions* must be made.

This process operates at home as well as in offices and organizations. Tasks in the home must be organized. The supplies needed for seeding and watering the lawn must be planned for and obtained in time. The appropriate person or persons in the family to whom the task will be assigned must be identified. The instructions must be specific. (The son of one of the authors, nine years old at the time, nearly killed a young fir tree by taking too seriously his father's admonition, "Fritz, that tree needs shaping. Go ahead and trim it." Not only was the tree trimmed, it was reduced to about half its original size!) Periodic checks on the progress of the seeding project will be needed, as well as rational decision making regarding type of grass seed and when to fertilize, water, and cut.

Summing up how she delegates, Phyllis Graff Culp, a seminar development coordinator, says, "Delegation for me involves identifying persons with the necessary skills, giving them careful instructions (and training, if necessary) plus clear expectations of the project development and completion." Management (no matter in what setting it takes place) is indeed a process—a series of interrelated activities. And, of these various activities, delegation is one of the most demanding and rewarding of all!

9

AVOIDING
INTERRUPTIONS

Time is a dressmaker specializing in alterations.

FAITH BALDWIN

Interruptions Kill Time

Three of the world's outstanding time studies confirm that managers are interrupted on the average every eight minutes all day long.[1] While most managers are dimly aware that interruptions are a problem, they are shocked when they

---

[1] Sune Carlson, *Executive Behavior: A Study of the Workload and Working Methods of Managing Directors* (Stockholm: Strombergs, 1951); Stewart, Rosemary, *Managers and Their Jobs* (Pan Books Limited, 1967); Luijk, D. H., *Waar Blijft de Tijd van de Directeur?* N. Samsom n.v.—uitgeyer—Alhpen aan den Rijn.

discover by taking a time log the extent to which their typical day is fragmented.

In our studies of timewasters, we see that a majority of them represent some form of interruption. In the following list of the world's top eight timewasters, an asterisk has been placed before those representing an obvious (*) or implied (**) interruption:

   * Telephone interruptions
   * Crises
     Lack of objectives, priorities, planning
   * Drop-in visitors
  ** Ineffective delegation
  ** Attempting too much at once
   * Meetings
   * Personal disorganization, cluttered desk

In other chapters we discuss the time that is wasted by not knowing clearly what your objectives and priorities are or by not being organized. An equally devastating toll of time is taken by unrelenting interruptions, unless you can find ways to control them.

Causes of Interruptions

Superficial remedies are risky, unless you find the real causes. Solutions hastily arrived at may solve one obvious cause but leave unsolved, or even aggravated, other less obvious but equally serious causes. For example, across-the-board budget cuts deserve their reputation as the work of an unprofessional manager for this very reason—the best programs are cut equally with the worst. A more effective manager would likely have eliminated the worst programs while *increasing* the budget of the best programs.

An examination of interruptions yields two broad categories which are helpful in determining causes. We think first, and often only, of *externally* generated interruptions. The incoming phone call which interrupts a conference or thinking through a problem, the drop-in neighbor who may simply be whiling away time, the unexpected crisis due to oversights of others, the unscheduled meeting, and the like, illustrate this kind. Some intriguing questions will be explored later concerning how such external interruptions can be encouraged by one's own actions (such as leaving your door open). Nevertheless, it is clear that these interruptions arise through actions of others and are events which appear at first glance to be outside of your control, or "externally generated."

An additional category of interruptions is "internally generated." Examples include leaving tasks unfinished, inability to say no, indecision, procrastination, personal disorganization, and lack of self-discipline. These all interrupt completion of tasks and are self-generated.

When we analyze these interruptions for specific causes, again we find that some are externally caused and others are internally generated.

External causes of interruptions range from working in a crisis-prone business or agency to an overcurious, overcontrolling, or insecure boss or board president. Lack of a secretary or an assistant ranks high, along with overdependent or untrained staff or an inadequate phone system. Physical location (next to the front door, vending machine, or rest rooms) can also produce external interruptions.

Among the important *internal* causes of interruptions are *ego* (only *I* can answer their questions), *fear of offending* (if I don't answer my own phone), *desire to appear available* (call me, or drop in any time), and *being interruption-prone* due to short attention span, insecurity, or a dislike for your work.

Importance of Principles

A woman concerned about controlling interruptions needs to know not only *what* to do, but *why*, so that if conditions change she will be able to revise or adapt her actions to the new situation. Knowing the principles involved enables her to be successful indefinitely by developing solutions to changing problems.

Principle of Planned Unavailability

This has been developed to deal with interruptions. Reducing the number, duration, and impact of interruptions increases accomplishment. Techniques for controlling interruptions include screening calls and visitors, completing tasks before permitting interruptions, testing the legitimacy of interruptions by questions such as "Can it wait?" or "Could someone else help?" and planning for periods of limited unavailability by utilizing a "quiet hour" or a hideaway.

Women must plan for periods of uninterrupted concentration. The mistaken notion that you should always be accessible may lead to such abuses as the ever-open door which stands as a continuing invitation to drop in for a visit—to passersby and corridor-wanderers at the office and to family members and neighbors at home—whether or not they have anything important in mind.

Principle of Tyranny of the Urgent

Most women live in constant tension between the urgent and the important. Urgent tasks call for instant action and drive the important from your consciousness. You may feel tyrannized by the urgent and consequently respond unwittingly to the endless pressures of the moment, neglecting the long-term consequences of more important but less demanding tasks left undone.

Principle of Indecision

The arrival at the point of decision causes many women (without apparent reason) to hesitate, vacillate, or refuse to decide. Indecision should be viewed as a decision *not* to decide. Like procrastination, this simply postpones the ultimate decision, which will occasion a later interruption when that time occurs. We need to recognize that the ability to make up our minds conclusively is vital as a counter to hesitation, vacillation, and procrastination. On the other hand, good judgment warns that when decisions are made hastily, impulsively, or without adequate thought, this also causes interruptions later on when corrective measures are required. Discipline yourself to get the critical facts and to decide without undue delay.

Remember too that in any group setting decisions should be made at the lowest level where appropriate information and judgment exist, in order to save management time. This theory applies in families, too. Leave as many of their decisions as possible to the children, again where appropriate information and judgment exist.

Principle of Procrastination

Deferring, postponing, or putting off decisions or actions can become a costly habit—losing time, wasting opportunities, increasing pressure of deadlines, and generating crises. Like indecision, procrastination necessitates an interruption later on to make the decision or take the action. So discipline yourself to take the action—or make the decision—*now*.

An understanding of relevant principles of management yields the bonus of knowing that (1) the actions one is taking to solve a problem are not only the obvious ones, but that (2) they are also the right ones. Any businesswoman or housewife has thought, for example, how nice it would be to close her door so she could get something done without incessant interruptions. Had she just known that the powerful principle of interruption control was valid—that it's *all right* to limit phone calls and drop-in visitors—she needn't have felt guilty over it. After all, the "open-door" policy was only intended to signal accessibility, not necessarily to mean keeping the door physically open *all* of the time, and it can be modified to suit the situation.

Eight Steps to Fewer Interruptions

Some solutions to interruptions are so relevant to other aspects of time management that they are dealt with in other chapters, but for reinforcement let us mention the important ones here:

1. *Set aside a "quiet hour" each day.* Should you leave your door open at all times so colleagues will have easy access to you, and so you will be viewed as a cooperative, responsive member of the team . . . or should you close it some of the time, providing yourself needed privacy to get your job done? Or at home, should you *always* be available to *everyone*?

A few years ago the belief prevailed that women *should* be available to others on demand. And many organizations adopted the open-door policy for both men and women. If you were a "team player," you were always available!

Unfortunately, it is a myth that an open-door policy always improves leadership or effectiveness. In fact, it can destroy it, if used indiscriminantly. Experiments have shown how difficult it is for a person to walk by a friend's or associate's open door without a greeting. Given the average person's instinct for socializing, curiosity for "the latest," fear of offending, or desire to be popular—the open door is actually a serious threat to effective management. Mark Dundon, former administrator of St. Charles Hospital in Toledo, studied the impact of the open-door policy on his administrative team. Evaluation of their time logs indicated that random unplanned interruptions resulting from the policy wasted one and a half hours daily on the average for *each member* of the team. By modifying the policy and preplanning most of their meetings, they each saved over one hour daily by avoiding unnecessary interruptions.

Experts agree that for a portion of each day you need time alone, if at all possible. Pick a "quiet hour" or "closed-door" time—an uninterrupted period you can count on for thinking, planning, or finishing a high-priority task. Alert the people around you that that's the time when you are not to be interrupted except for some emergency. So long as others have that prior information, almost all business they have to transact with you can be handled either before or after your private hour. At the office, if you have a secretary, he or she can become skilled at taking callbacks: "Yes, she's in, but unavailable just now. Can I help you, or can she call you back when she's free?" Some managers report that one daily quiet hour accomplished so much for them that they have initiated a second one!

Secretaries who are fortunate enough to have someone with whom they can trade off have accomplished miracles too by trading quiet hours—taking each other's phone calls or other interruptions while they catch up on a backlog or get out material for a boss's deadline. At home, housewives can request their friends not to call them at a certain time of day (one woman we know asks them not to call before noon for social chats). Some mothers have taught their children not to interrupt them at certain times which are "reserved for Mother."

The quiet hour enables women to get three hours of regular work done in one, assuming they are well organized. No single technique will increase a woman's effectiveness more for the invested time, while saving her up to two hours a day!

2. *Screen phone calls and visitors*. A professional secretary who screens calls and visitors often gets answers faster for the callers, while saving time for the manager. Confirmed emergencies and VIPs are, of course, treated on that basis, but for routine calls either the secretary or others on the staff should be well qualified to either handle them at once or get the answers and call back, if necessary. Skillful handling by an experienced secretary will usually expedite answers compared with waiting for the boss to call back. This action saves many managers one to two hours per day, without offending anyone. This often calls for "credentializing" the secretary by telling associates or clients that he or she will be handling their questions, and that this secretary is well qualified to do so. The secretary or receptionist should be located close enough to your door to screen the casual, drop-in visitor: "Hello, Bill, what can I do for you?" is an excellent opener, because it gets to the business at hand immediately and courteously. The secretary will probably be able to answer many questions of the inveterate "dropper-in."

When the time and place are right for you to make and return phone calls, don't allow other interruptions to interfere. Stay with the telephoning long enough to ensure a sense of accomplishment for yourself. (Mary Kay Ash, keeps a three-minute timer by her phone. "I also write down the points I need to cover before making each call," she reports.)

3. *Learn to say no without offending*. This technique applies to interruptions almost across the board. The endless requests of others for help or information on projects not within a woman's current ability to respond require some sort of defense which will not offend. Remember the four steps in saying no (described in Chapter 3) which will virtually ensure no offense to others:

a. *Listen* to ensure understanding and convey sympathy.

b. *Say no immediately* to eliminate doubt and the guilt which continued discussion engenders.

c. *Give reasons* so that it can be accepted.

d. *Offer alternatives* to demonstrate good faith. Example: "I understand, Jim, why you want me to be in the meeting at four. I'm sorry, but there's no way I can be there. You see, I have a project deadline this afternoon. If you'd like I'll give you my reaction to the proposal right now. Then you'll know my position." Or, perhaps, for some ongoing project, you can agree to discuss it the next morning.

4. *Delegate.* One reason for many interruptions is the failure of managers to delegate effectively. Unclear instructions, for example, necessitate later interruptions for clarification or correction. Selection of incompetent or untrained subordinates will require the same. Failure to delegate also prevents the screening party, who has the responsibility, from rerouting the interrupting party to others.

5. *Limit your involvement in:*

a. *Meetings.* Attend only those meetings where your presence is required and then, if possible, for only as long as you are really needed (see Chapter 10). By avoiding an unnecessary meeting you are avoiding an unnecessary interruption . . . which may last a lot longer than you thought it would!

b. *Crises.* Don't overreact. Don't treat every problem as a crisis. Ignore those that have peaked. Sometimes attention at an inopportune time only fans the flames. Delegate crises which others can handle. Get involved only where your presence is required, and then only to the extent necessary.

c. *Routine and Detail.* Do nothing you can delegate. Stay uninvolved with routine and matters of detail.

d. *Tasks already delegated.* Once you've delegated a task, don't take it back or get involved in it unless necessary. Resist upward delegation.

6. *Do it to a finish.* When you drop one thing to do another, you have interrupted yourself. Don't put a project down unfinished if you can avoid it. It may take more time to refamiliarize yourself with a project than to finish it as expeditiously as possible on the first handling. Resist the temptation to leave tasks unfinished.

7. *Handle it once.* Do not put items back in the in-box or on your desk if you can dispose of them the first time. Eighty percent of the items which come to your attention *can* be disposed of on the first handling. Yet, the average woman *actually* disposes of approximately 20 percent on the first handling. Thus indecision and procrastination are encouraged, desks become cluttered, letters and memos are shuffled and reshuffled, paperwork goes home in briefcases which return unopened. Documents are lost, and retrieval time for missing items takes an ever-increasing toll.

8. *Keep your desktop clear.* Perhaps the most costly timewaster of all is the items left on the desk so they won't be forgotten. In fact they are remembered each time your gaze alights on them. As we mentioned in Chapter 7, concentration is broken, and momentum and continuity are lost. Frustration over the mounting pile of unfinished work increases. You're no longer running your job—it is running you. If you *could* dispose of 80 percent of those items on first handling, but *actually* dispose of only 20 percent of it, you're only being 25 percent effective!

Too Little Time—or Too Many Interruptions?

Since you already have all the time there is, why not plan for it to be enough? Make sure the time you have is enough to get the important things—your real priorities—done. Recognize the unprecedented power of interruptions to kill time, and by controlling them save up to two hours a day. This will help you finish what really needs doing and also allow you to do those things you've never found time for but would really enjoy.

10

MAKING MEETINGS COUNT!

. . . nobody is of the same opinion nobody means the
same thing by what they say as the other one means
and only the one who is talking thinks he means what
he is saying even though he knows very well that that
is not what he is saying.

GERTRUDE STEIN

Compared with other skill-building approaches for women,
conference leadership—the management of meetings—has
escaped the scrutiny of most authors and lecturers until recently. Now a spate of books, articles, and seminars attests
to its arrival on the self-development scene. It is a subject
which can no longer be ignored by those aspiring to succeed.

For women, successful conference leadership or participation can pose special problems. Depending upon the
situation, these problems may range from your excessive

timidity as a participant to subtle and often overt resistance to you as the leader.

In this chapter we will examine time-wasting problems that meetings pose in general and those that may be especially troublesome for women in particular.

Potential Timewasters in Meetings

1. Purpose: May be unclear, not understood by everyone.
2. Plan/Agenda: Often ignored—with disastrous results in wasted time.
3. People: Often people are there who don't need to be, and therefore shouldn't be, or people who should be there and are missing.
4. Place and Space: May be inadequate or exposed to distractions.
5. Time Dimensions: Most meetings start late and end late.
6. Leadership—Climate: Every meeting has a "feeling." If positive, fine; if not, the convenor needs the skill of easing a tense, possibly hostile atmosphere into a cooperative one as quickly as possible.
7. Leadership—Conducting the Meeting: Conference leadership is a vital skill for almost all of us. It can be learned.
8. Follow-up: Follow-up is essential to ensure that decisions are carried out. If no decisions were called for, were the intended purposes of the meeting accomplished?
9. Costs: Most meetings cost money—for supplies, resource people, space. And *all* meetings cost time—the cost in people's time as measured by their compensation and, often, time lost in ill-advised or unnecessary meetings.[1]

[1] Eva Schindler-Rainman, and Ronald Lippitt, *Taking Your Meetings Out of the Doldrums* (Columbus, Ohio: APD, 1975), pp. 27ff.

Nine out of ten managers polled in time management seminars over a ten-year period reported that *at least* half their time spent in meetings is wasted. Those of you in management positions are estimated to spend two hours per day in meetings, suggesting an average of *one hour per day* wasted by most!

What can be done to cut this time loss in meetings?

Purpose

There should be a bona fide *need* before a meeting is called. Of course, many do have a real purpose: to coordinate activities, to disseminate urgent information, to reach a consensus or decision, to solve a problem, build morale, etc.

But there are other meetings which should not occur at all. Among them are those a project director or department head calls because she is unwilling to make a risky decision alone and wants support (or shared blame, if things turn out badly!). Or she may call a meeting to "know everything" in case the boss asks or to satisfy an ego need to demonstrate "I'm in charge." Another example is the "I want everyone in this meeting" syndrome—an insecure leader who involves others without regard to *their* priorities *or* the real need to have them in the meeting. Then there is the leader who, when confronted with a disciplinary problem and in order to avoid direct confrontation, will involve others' time to give herself added psychological protection. Crisis situations often generate meetings to solve problems which should never have occurred or which could have been solved without calling a meeting.

Some of us have a compulsion toward overcommunication: We call meetings for the sake of meetings! This meeting-itis syndrome destroyed the morale of a major division of an international food corporation. A vice-president of the division showed us one of her monthly calendars with shaded areas indicating an array of half- and full-day staff meetings with her boss. *Forty percent* of her working time that month was spent in meetings called by an insecure boss plying his team with questions to prepare himself for top corporate meetings in which he feared being asked questions he might not be able to answer!

The most common unnecessary meeting is the too-frequently scheduled "regular" staff meeting. A president of an international airline met daily with his top team for over an hour without an agenda. Then, following a time management seminar, these meetings were compressed to weekly one-hour sessions with a preset agenda. This resulted in a savings of nearly *one hour per day* for *each* of the top ten people in this 5000-person organization!

TO ATTEND . . . OR NOT?   It is legitimate to avoid attending meetings when the purpose is unclear. If you need a reason not to attend such a meeting, use your own priorities and deadlines. For example, you might say, "Bill, when the reason for the meeting is clarified, let me know. If I'm needed, I'll surely try to be there. Meanwhile I'm facing some priority deadlines."

If you are asked to attend a meeting not directly related to your needs, instead of attending, you might ask for a copy of the minutes or send a report or a representative. If you do go, stay only for the portion that is relevant to you. If you are to give a report, ask for the specific time you will be needed and get prior agreement to speak and leave—or ask if you can speak first. Or ask a subordinate to attend and report back. This gives your team experience and also saves your time.

TO CALL A MEETING . . . OR NOT?   How can a woman determine whether a meeting she's planning is necessary? She should clarify the purpose and then ask herself whether she could achieve that same purpose by (1) some delegation or action on her own, (2) a written communication to one or more persons, (3) one or more phone calls, or (4) even a conference call. (See Appendix for a conference-call agenda form.)

If someone else is asking her to call a meeting, if appropriate she can encourage that person to go ahead with the decision without wasting others' time in a meeting. She can further encourage persons to do their own problem solving by writing down the problem and suggesting their own answers before asking for help.

Calling meetings may pose a problem for a woman manager with any subordinate, male *or* female, who is resisting her authority. Being called to a meeting, especially if there is little or no notice, can upset plans and interrupt priorities for those being called. A clear statement of purpose, so long as it is recognized as a priority item, may defuse this resistance. It could also provide specifics to be used as reasons for *not* attending. The effective leader will be ready with the reason(s) requiring personal attendance and will announce the meeting well in advance to minimize the anticipated excuse of conflicting schedules.

WHEN YOU DO CALL A MEETING? Have the purpose pinned down clearly. What is needed: a decision? a consensus? to build morale? to disseminate information and if so, about what?

Make sure the purpose is clearly spelled out and specific. Is it to discuss the staff reorganization plan or setting objectives for next year? Then get more specific. For example, don't say that the meeting is being held to "talk about next year's finances." Rather, it is to "prioritize and assign a dollar figure to each of the line items in the $50,000 'career development budget.'" Now you are ready to make out an agenda, decide whom to call, and assign responsibility for the preparations.

Plan/Agenda

The airline president mentioned previously was totally unaware of the time being wasted in his own meetings due to
the lack of an agenda. According to those attending, they
spent the first half of each daily meeting trying to determine
whether there was anything important enough to be discussed. The rest of the time they spent either disagreeing or
sharing their ignorance, since no one could come prepared.

The best way to prevent this kind of timewasting is for
the convenor to prepare an agenda of the items which *need* to
be discussed. List them in order of their importance. Screen
them on the basis of concern to all; perhaps some could be
assigned to a committee for those few involved to decide
themselves. Limit the agenda to the items that can be given
adequate attention during the time allowed.

Make sure that critical information is available, and that
the agenda is set and distributed in advance. If advisable,
send copies to persons who do not necessarily need to attend
but do need to know what is being discussed and by whom.
This permits a judgment as to whether they wish to attend
or to make their views known in advance. The meeting
agenda in Figure 1 is a sample of the kind of agenda which
will be most helpful to all the participants.

TIME-LIMIT YOUR AGENDA. The time-limited agenda
allocates time to various subjects according to their relative
priority. For example, thirty minutes may be allocated to
topic A, twenty minutes to topic B, and ten minutes to topic
C. This permits busy participants who might not be needed
for the whole meeting to know when the items which concern them will come up, and for how long, so they can plan
to attend the portion which is of interest to them. It provides
leverage for those in the meeting to limit potential time overruns on early topics at the expense of later ones. A participant can now say, "The time for this item is up. Can we
move to the next one?"

Figure 1

MEETING AGENDA

Date: _____ Time: _____ Location: _____

Persons to attend: Responsible for items:
1.
2.
3.
4.

Approx. Time	Item	Decision	Person Responsible	Deadline
————	1. _____ Points to Consider a. b. c.			
————	2. _____ Points to Consider a. b. c.			
————	3. _____ Points to Consider a. b. c.			

   This technique assures that time will be devoted to topics according to priority. This avoids fulfilling Parkinson's little-known Second Law: that time in meetings is usually spent on subjects in inverse relation to their importance.

   Two examples underscore the problems encountered when not using a time-limiting agenda. One is a church in a Chicago suburb whose board of trustees was meeting to make the final decision on a $350,000 budget. Someone brought up the quality of the paper towels used in the kitchen and rest rooms. The ensuing discussion lasted for thirty-five minutes and was only halted when one elder realized she would have to leave in fifteen minutes! The trustees consequently discussed the budget itself for fifteen minutes (granted, it had been considered previously) and voted final approval on one-third of a million dollars! The pastor later cited it as an example of misplaced emphasis— "35 minutes on paper towels, and 15 minutes on our annual budget."

Likewise, the twenty busy doctors on the board of directors of a large medical center met *three different times* to discuss the removal or bracing of a large tree which had split in a storm and was endangering the building. By the time they decided they did *not* have the expertise needed and called in an expert, the incomes of the twenty doctors, prorated over the time spent on the tree, far exceeded the sizable cost of its removal!

In each of these cases, a time-limited agenda and an alert chairperson could have averted such a waste of time.

PRESET YOUR STARTING AND ENDING TIME.   Announce the starting and ending times for your meeting. This permits others to plan their own day around your meeting. If some items can't be dealt with, those left over will be less important ones and can be taken up another time. Just in case there *might* be time left over, be prepared with some additional items that may need to be dealt with sometime. Then decide whether to utilize the extra time discussing additional topics or, even better, adjourn early so everyone gains extra time for more important personal priorities.

People
Only those with a *need to attend* should be invited.

Some are invited as a courtesy, others because they expect to be. Some are asked to attend "in case something comes up on which they may have some information, or may need to know about." (Often they could be called when or if they *are* really needed, or a specific question for clarification or confirmation could be relayed to them later.)

Some meetings scheduled to inform, motivate, reach a consensus, or persuade may need to include the whole team. However, for many others designed to solve a problem, set priorities, or define long-range objectives, only those directly responsible for the decision should be taken away from their work.

The more people attending a meeting, the more difficult it can become to achieve a consensus. As described by Hensleigh Wedgwood,

The larger the group, the greater the difficulty in establishing communication among the individuals in it. In a "group" of two, communication is comparatively easy, because there are only two communication channels. But add a third person to this group and you immediately set up six channels. Add a fourth and you have twelve; get eight people together and you have 56 channels to sort out and so on.

It follows that the larger the size of the group, the less likelihood there is of utilizing fully the resources of its individual members and the less control the Chairman will be able to exercise in bringing the meeting to a consensus or any resolution of the problems it has set out to solve.[2]

People who aren't needed should, in fact, be discouraged from coming. If they are needed for a limited contribution, their time could be scheduled so they can make it and then leave to get back to their work. Many contributions could be made adequately by a subordinate, a memo, or over the telephone.

Remember, each nonessential attendee is wasting his or her time *and*, of course, money for each minute unnecessarily spent in a meeting instead of on the job.

THE NUANCES OF POWER. There can be "power" nuances inherent in deciding who attends meetings. The effective woman will be sensitive to these nuances and their

---

[2] Hensleigh Wedgwood, "Fewer Camels, More Horses," *Personnel*, July–August 1967.

implications for other individuals on her team. In cases where resistance to her authority is a problem, she'll find that her strict adherence to principles of equitable treatment and evenhanded firmness with group members will be rewarded.

For some insecure women (and men), attendance at meetings may be mistakenly viewed as a badge of success. Conversely, it may also be viewed as "being sent because you need it" when applied to training seminars.

Women with an image problem may be especially prone to insecurity about nonattendance at meetings. They are afraid of missing out on something, of not being invited, or of not being thought important enough to be called. The mature, professional woman recognizes these traps and avoids them. Simply asking for a copy of the minutes should suffice if the outcome has possible, if not significant, relevance to your work.

Much has been written to advise women where to sit and how to conduct themselves as effective participants in meetings called by others. Our caution is not to overdo your concern about this. Common sense is the best criterion.

NOT WASTING TIME WHEN REQUIRED TO ATTEND IRRELEVANT MEETINGS. Tuning out of required meetings *when nothing relevant to her is going on* has helped a woman manager in Toronto utilize this time which was previously wasted. Instead of becoming hopelessly bored, she would think through a problem, organize her day, and plan next steps, all while apparently listening. Another woman, a prominent elected official, made out her entire Christmas list while sitting through a particularly boring interagency meeting.

Place and Space

A less than adequate location (sometimes even an impossible one!) and the failure to anticipate equipment needs are frequent deterrents to running a meeting smoothly. Fortunate is the woman who has not yet found herself in such a predicament!

If the room is too noisy, badly ventilated, or too small to meet the needs of the group, the meeting organizer won't hear the last of it for a long time. "Who picked this room?" "Is this the best you can do, Susie?" "When you come up in the ranks a little you'll learn better" are samples of the ribbing she may get. Worse still, if she lost a better room because she hadn't reserved it and someone else got there first, she might be reminded less subtly that if she had a little clout such things wouldn't happen.

Be sure that the lighting and seating are adequate. If there will be writing to do, will everyone have a writing surface? Are there electrical outlets for audiovisual equipment, and room to use visual aids? If unfamiliar with the meeting space, visit it yourself and determine the best arrangement: how close or how far you want the participants seated from each other and the leader, and also the level of comfort desired—not enough and the members could become grouchy or restless, too much and the meeting may lapse into irrelevancies and dozing. Legend has it that a well-known company became concerned over excessive amounts of time being wasted in long meetings. They had two inches cut off the front legs of the chairs in their conference room to lower the comfort level. Meetings became noticeably shorter.

If visual aids are being used, have them set up *ahead of time*. Make sure the equipment is in good running order and that the operator (especially if it is you) is familiar with it. This is particularly important for women because a woman can be doubly embarrassed if the projector or tape recorder doesn't work properly. The old messages are reinforced: "Just like a woman—can't even run a simple machine" or "If she can't handle that piece of equipment, how can she possibly handle this new job assignment?!"

Occasionally you might be expected to handle a larger meeting with outside resource people or consultants involved. Contact them well ahead of time to be sure they are available, and clear as to their role and input. It is always wise to confirm arrangements with busy people the day before. Finalize arrangements for equipment if the meeting is to be recorded in any way other than secretary's minutes, such as audio tape, video, or television. If there are special visitors, observers, or media personnel attending, have someone briefed and ready to assist them, complete with name tags if indicated.

FOR OUT-OF-TOWN MEETINGS. Occasionally, a woman will find herself responsible for a larger meeting outside her own organization, and even in another city. In such a case all the above-mentioned concerns pertain, with a few additional ones. Ascertain far ahead of time what hotels or public buildings have the facilities you need and how convenient they are to transportation. Can they take care of all services required? Are lodging and meals available close at hand? Can they furnish all the props you need, including electronic ones? Pin down the reservations with plenty of time to spare.

When meeting rooms must be selected before the number of attendees can be known, it is better to err on the side of too large a room than too small. Like all professional lecturers who do not control all their speaking sites, the authors feel they have encountered their share of difficult situations. In Hong Kong, for example, 125 chief executives appeared for a meeting in a room designed to hold 75! Fortunately they were high-spirited young executives who rose to the occasion, crowded into corners, sat on the floor, in the aisles, and outside three doors so all could hear!

There are meeting rooms with posts in the center which block visibility, no soundproof partitions for adjoining rooms, audiovisual equipment which doesn't work or projection screens which collapse. Adjacent noise can range from the film in the next meeting room tuned so loud that your own people are distracted, to the bugles of a sales convention with which each of twenty-five award-winning salespeople were once welcomed to the platform.

For contingencies it is well to keep a permanent list against which to check the various types of seating arrangements, platform props, kinds of equipment, and even refreshments which your organization expects for larger meetings. Happy is the woman who can pull a spare projector bulb or extension cord out of her hat in an emergency, too! Remember Murphy's Third Law: "If anything *can* go wrong, it will," and try to forestall any possible disasters before they occur.

Time Dimensions

How much time will your meeting require? Seldom does anything short of a full-blown conference *need* to last more than an hour. If half an hour should suffice, plan for that and make every effort to conclude within that framework. Would a stand-up meeting do? Charles E. Wilson, renowned for his mobilization of American industry in World War I, was also famed for his ten-minute meetings. He started on the dot, hastened to the point, reached a decision, and adjourned the meeting. Arriving late, many of his managers found themselves responsible for something about which they had missed all the details! Often, when co-workers stopped Wilson in hallways to suggest a meeting on some matter, Wilson replied, "We're here now, let's decide!"

CHOOSE THE TIME WISELY. It is poor judgment to call a meeting at a time when certain key people or some critical information may not be available. Meetings strategically set for half an hour before lunch or quitting time are more likely to go briskly. Eyes on the clock spur concentrated effort and discourage irrelevant though interesting side ventures.

SEND OUT NOTICES IN ADVANCE. Advise participants what is expected of the meeting—and of them—far enough in advance to allow adequate preparation. A handy form for making those expectations clear, *a meeting notice*, is shown in Figure 2. Include both starting and ending times.

START AND STOP ON TIME! To discourage overruns of meetings *start on time, get and stick to the point, respect time limits* for the agenda items, achieve your *objective,* and *end on time*. Remember, there is no substitute for any of these things if your meetings are to be successful!

Leadership–Improving the Climate

Too often, the leader of a meeting has taken little time to think about how to ensure the atmosphere she wants. Antagonistic feelings may develop because the purpose of the meeting is misunderstood, the method of notification is inadequate, attendance is compulsory when not really needed,

Figure 2

NOTICE OF MEETING

Group: _____

Subject/Agenda: _____

Date: _____

Place: _____

Beginning time: _____

Closing time: _____

Materials to be read ahead of time: _____

_____

Materials to be brought to the meeting: _____

_____

and personalities tangle because of a chance remark or an imagined slight.

Women in general are more sensitive than men to these elements of a successful meeting, and women are often more skilled in easing tense situations into more cooperative and productive ones. A bit of humor, a friendly question, a diversionary comment with a light touch, or shifting to another subject may be all that is needed. When personal animosity or opposition to a desired project is known, try having a friendly meeting with the antagonist at a coffee break, over the phone, or at dinner in order to win cooperation ahead of the meeting or to disarm the personal unfriendliness. Time and hassling in many a meeting has been saved by such diplomacy.

Women who must chair many meetings may find resources such as "Group Blocking Roles" and "Group Supporting Roles" by Wedgwood[3] helpful in developing skill in handling difficult situations and keeping the meeting on track.

Leadership–Conducting the Meeting

START THE MEETING ON TIME! By waiting for latecomers, we penalize those who come on time and reward those who come late. Before long, everyone will automatically arrive late.

"But how do you get people here on time?" The answer is always "By starting on time." As long as the leader allows late starts the proceedings will *never* start on time. The authors know of a meeting that was called on time, started on time, and ended fifteen minutes later, several critical decisions having been made that affected areas of *tardy* mem-

---

[3] Hensleigh Wedgwood, "Fewer Camels, More Horses," *Personnel,* July–August 1967.

bers' responsibilities. The tardy members were on time after
that!

GET AND STICK TO THE POINT.   Many meetings are
painfully slow getting to the point. This, of course, is a
matter of leadership, with the agenda needing to be before
everyone. The chairperson who accepts deviation from the
agenda, who allows a topic-jumper to change the subject, or
worse, who herself leads the discussion astray, is performing a great disservice to all.

Some women may have more trouble refereeing this
problem than men because of reluctance to assert leadership
over men. But there are appropriate ways to get the discussion back on track. Example: "That's an interesting obser-
vation, Bill. Now, are there any other comments on the
matter before we proceed to the next point?" Intelligent,
aware, and objective-oriented leadership is demonstrated by
those women who successfully chair meetings of mixed
groups.

An introduction or summary *before* handing out related
materials can save time. If you don't do it then, people will
be skimming materials while you're talking. This is a particularly relevant issue for women, because it is an additional way in which you can establish your competence in
the eyes of others. If you are concise and well prepared in
your verbal summary, and you have the group's full attention as you present yourself and your material, your credibil-
ity increases. Another option: If the agenda is in front of
people from the time the meeting starts, you can present it
as a brief, concise summary of the purpose and objectives of
the meeting.

A "minutes remaining" clock or a "timekeeper" can
speed up discussions. When people are aware that the remaining time is waning, they are more likely to be efficient in

their use of that time. A well-known superintendent of schools in New York State uses this with excellent results. Interruptions are kept to a minimum. Messages are held for break times, except for cases of confirmed emergencies.

INVOLVE EVERYONE.   Involving reluctant participants is important in any group. This can be done by asking, "John, what do you see as our biggest problem in this project?" or "Mary, are you in favor of this budget change?" The opposite problem also can occur if someone is dominating the discussion. A comment such as "Charlie, those are interesting ideas. How do some of the rest of you feel?" can often retrieve control. It strengthens the conduct of most meetings if the leader remains neutral.

ACHIEVE YOUR OBJECTIVE.   While watching the time is *very* important, not only for each meeting but also to set a pattern for the group, remember you are there for a purpose, and allow for some flexibility in time spent on specific agenda items. Blind adherence to a schedule, in the face of changing circumstances, could be very counterproductive.

END ON TIME.   Leave a few minutes before adjourning the meeting to summarize the decisions made. This focuses attention on the critical issues. Check that all assignments for needed committees or follow-up are made.

Close the meeting promptly. If there is resistance because of interest in items remaining to be discussed, the sensitive leader can suggest alternatives: perhaps a fifteen-minute meeting before lunch the next day or "If it can't wait until our next meeting, Bill, would you and Charlie like to come into my office to discuss it now?" As soon as participants see that the leader is serious about finishing on schedule, they will begin disciplining themselves to get the agenda covered in the designated time.

Of course, if ending on time becomes a fetish, one may sacrifice valuable discussion and new ideas for the sake of a few minutes. This could be false economy. Judgment must be exercised in all cases. One more note of caution: Some people, who simply don't believe in meetings at all, may *need* to call a few and be cautious about ending them prematurely. As in all aspects of leadership, much depends upon the situation.

Follow-up

GET THOSE MINUTES OUT! Concise minutes, listing the *decisions made*, the *responsibilities assigned for implementation*, and the *deadlines for action and follow-up* to be taken should be completed and distributed within twenty-four hours if possible, or forty-eight hours at the outside. Fuzzy, imprecise notes reviewing discussions are usually of little value and are best left out. One simple yet thorough form for minutes lists the identity of the group, the date, and those attending at the top of a sheet. Below this comes the summarizing, by item, of (1) the subject, (2) the decision, (3) responsibility (who is to handle), and (4) the deadline.

MONITOR PROGRESS OF ASSIGNMENTS. Monitoring assignment progress is advisable, at predetermined intervals. At the next meeting, unfinished business can be the first agenda item. Deadlines which have not been met are discussed. This helps ensure that the assignments will be completed on time!

Periodically, take a committee inventory, checking whether particular committees' objectives have been achieved, and if not, when they can be expected to be. Abolish those committees that have accomplished their intended purpose.

Costs

The responsible leader must have a realistic grasp of how costly meetings can be. Consider the total cost in salaries, fringe benefits (which can approximate one-third of the salaries), plus any other incidental costs of space, equipment, food, and beverages that may be involved. Add preparation costs of labor, printing materials, travel expense, and lost time before, during, and after the meeting. It is quite possible that one meeting could cost an organization three or more times as much as any savings gained through decisions made at that meeting!

Consider too the double loss to an organization if a meeting is called which is not needed, also keeping the participants from their own individual priorities. Example: A crisis arises because one manager has not developed a contingency plan for a problem situation; consequently, five high-level managers spend two hours each in a meeting to try to determine corrective measures for the emergency. Expensive time is wasted on a problem which should never have occurred *and* high-priority tasks of each of these managers have been needlessly delayed! Or again, suppose ten board members spend a morning on a series of details relating to an upcoming meeting, each detail of which should have been decided by only one. The reason was that no one wanted to take the risk alone—they wanted to share the risk. A waste of time and money! The same high cost pertains when there are unnecessary overruns in meetings. Responsible leadership is needed to curtail all of these timewasters, for they are often far more costly than any benefits the group might derive.

Special Issues as Women

For some women meetings can become a focal point for their own insecurities. Their female conditioning may admonish, "You're a woman, be accommodating . . . be po-

lite." "Don't speak up." "Defer to the men in the group."
And on and on. Sometimes the awareness of this conditioning is delayed; only after several meetings do you realize
that you encouraged the men to monopolize the discussion
by your reticence, nods of encouragement, and ready smile.
Becoming aware of these subtleties is a process which takes
time. Recognizing what holds you back from taking an
active role in meetings is the first step in modifying your
behavior.

There are some specific guidelines you can follow to
enhance the likelihood of being taken seriously. Whether
chairing a meeting or present as a participant, *be prepared*.
Have ALL the pertinent facts *well* in hand and organized, so
as to make any point you wish succinctly and effectively.
Be brief and to the point. This is vital to presenting yourself as effectively as possible. If appropriate, speak up
early in the meeting to show that you are interested and
expect to participate. Taking notes is a further way to
show your interest and commitment to the outcome of the
discussion.

Consider not only *what to say* but also *how to present
yourself* to the best advantage. Messages are conveyed not
only by words but also by the tone of voice and what we
communicate nonverbally. Keep your voice in a lower register, and breathe slowly and deeply. Avoid nervous gestur-
ing. These approaches help make you appear poised, even if
you don't feel it! The effective female leader avoids elaborate hairdos, distracting jewelry, and clothing which is tight,
provocative, or inappropriate to the norms of her colleagues. Common sense, as in all other matters, is the ultimate criterion.

As a participant in meetings, learn to recognize the
bases of power. Sit as near as possible to either the chairperson (the formal power) or whoever, by seniority or force
of personality, is another base of power. Seek to develop

personal relationships with them. If this approach is coupled with "doing your homework" on the agenda items and a genuine commitment to the work of the group, you can develop your own base of power. If you are being asked consistently to serve in a role subordinate to a male equal, gaining the respect of the older members who assign the tasks is the first step to changing this. It is always possible that on the side you can request some responsibilities you know you can handle. If chauvinistic remarks keep coming, like "Will you take notes, Nancy?" or "Do you suppose there's any coffee left in the machine, hon?" respond to the specific situation. Either oblige gracefully and be prepared to make your contribution even in the midst of such services, or decide how to confront the situation assertively at the time or later on. "Since I took my turn last time, perhaps someone else could do it this time" may be the appropriate comment. If an additional reason seems appropriate, you could add: "I have several things to be catching up on in the meantime." In either case, be sure your input on the issue or task being discussed is worthy of attention, and respect will grow.

Avoid personalizing criticism. A common complaint about women is that they "take everything personally." A first step in letting go of this tendency is to avoid personalizing criticism toward others. Rather than "Katy, you're all wrong on that approach!" a better rejoinder would be "Katy, I suggest we consider a different approach to this problem." The woman who is likely to be chairing a number of meetings would do well to learn how to sense and handle subtle put-downs, and how to cope if her meeting place or hour is preempted by a male co-worker.

You can be an effective member of any decision-making group. Doing your homework, being creative in your thinking, and managing your contributions in meetings sensibly are key ingredients in *making meetings count*!

21 RULES FOR GETTING MORE FROM MEETINGS

Before Meeting

1. Generate alternatives: (a) decision, (b) conference call, (c) postpone, (d) cancel, (e) send a representative.
2. Define purpose clearly (to analyze, decide, inform, coordinate).
3. Limit attendance (only those needed should attend).
4. Stagger attendance (attend only for time needed to make contribution).
5. Pick right time (strategic timing—when information and attendees are available).
6. Pick right place (remote to avoid interruptions; geographically accessible).
7. Send advance agenda and information (no surprises—all prepared).
8. Compute cost per minute (measure cost of starting late and topic discussion).
9. Time-limit agenda by topic (apportion time in accordance with importance).
10. Time-limit meeting (establish and advise ending time).

During Meeting

11. Start on time (don't penalize those arriving on time and reward latecomers by waiting for them!).
12. Assign time-keeping and minutes responsibility.
13. Hold "stand-up" meetings.
14. Start with and stick to agenda. Style of leadership for chairperson may vary depending upon purpose of meeting—to inform, generate creative solutions, or decide.
15. Prevent interruptions (no phone calls or messages short of extreme emergencies).
16. Accomplish purpose. Restate conclusions. Clarify assignments.
17. Evaluate meeting (Was advance information adequate? Did meeting start on time? Was agenda followed and purpose achieved within time allocated? Were right people in attendance? Was time wasted?).
18. End on time (respect plans of those who assumed meeting would end on time).

After Meeting

19. Expedite minutes (concise minutes should include any decisions, those responsible, and deadlines; distribute within 48 hours).
20. Follow-up: (a) progress reports, (b) execution of decisions.
21. Take inventory of committees. Terminate those which have achieved their purpose.

11

ASSERTION . . . A TIMESAVER

What could love, the unsolved mystery, count for in face of this possession of self-assertion which she suddenly recognized as the strongest impulse of her being!

KATE CHOPIN (1889)

Assertiveness can lessen or eliminate some of the most critical timewasters! By speaking up for your own rights without stepping on the rights of others, you can improve control of your time and also increase your effectiveness, particularly on the telephone, with drop-in visitors, in meetings, when delegating, and when saying no to unreasonable requests.

Self-assertion is a way of stating what you think and how you feel without minimizing the other person. It's different from aggressive behavior, which directly or indirectly discounts another. Assertion is also different from passive behavior, in which you take seriously the feelings and thoughts of others but not your own. Passive behavior often seems the easy way out at the time and yet always results in bad feelings about yourself later on. Often these bad feelings are related to mismanagement of your time.

Why Assertion?

We all misuse our time and generate frustration for ourselves in doing so. For example, Joyce has a meeting at one o'clock on the other side of town. It's noon now. She realizes that she had no breakfast this morning, so she needs to eat lunch before her meeting. She goes into a restaurant, looks around, sees that it's fairly busy, and sits down. The waitress walks by . . . a few minutes pass . . . the waitress walks by again . . . another few minutes pass. Joyce looks at her watch, feeling frustrated, realizing that time is getting away from her. The only real action she takes, though, is to gesture half-heartedly at the waitress across the room, trying to catch her attention. Finally, Joyce realizes that even if the waitress came over at this point, took her order and brought her the food, she wouldn't have time to eat and get to the meeting by one. So, Joyce leaves the restaurant with an empty stomach and also some bad feelings, primarily bad feelings about her own ineffectiveness in the situation. She has reacted in a passive, self-discounting way, not having acknowledged and spoken up for her own rights.

In contrast, Joyce might have chosen to deal with the same situation aggressively. The first or second time the waitress walked by her, Joyce might have reached out and grabbed the waitress's arm and said something like, "Listen, lady, I'm in a big hurry. Bring me the menu right away so I can give you my order and be out of here in twenty minutes! OK?" Obviously, by behaving in this way, Joyce would be taking into account her own right, the right to go

into a restaurant and be served. In the process, though, she
would be treating the waitress in a hostile, discounting manner. Although Joyce might get served, she would feel uncomfortable about her own behavior when she reflected on
the situation later. Aggressive behavior will sometimes get
us what we want in the short run. However, two negative
payoffs are virtually certain. First will be the hostility of the
other person, who will most likely be very angry over being
treated in a demeaning fashion. The second, and later one,
will be your own bad feelings about yourself and how you
behaved in that situation.

If there are negative payoffs in being either passive or
aggressive, did Joyce have any other option in dealing with
the situation in the restaurant? She did: the assertive option.
The first or second time the waitress walked by, Joyce could
have reached out and touched the arm of the waitress to get
her attention. Then Joyce could have said, "I see you're
really busy right now, and I do need to order." In that
statement, Joyce has done two things. She's taken the waitress's situation into account by acknowledging that she's
busy. In addition, Joyce has taken herself seriously by stating her own need to order lunch and be served.

It's important to remember that the payoff in being assertive is *not* that you always get what you want. There is no
theory or technique which will guarantee that—because
you're not in control of the behavior of others. However, when you're assertive in a series of situations, you
increase the likelihood of getting what you want most of the
time. The *positive payoff* in being assertive (and it's *always
there*!) is that you have good feelings about yourself both at
the time the situation is occurring and later on. When you're
assertive, you know you've done everything you can do.
You've taken the feelings and rights of the other person into
account, and you've also taken your own feelings and rights

seriously. That's a powerful positive payoff and will add immeasurably to a woman's self-esteem!

What Do I Do to Be More Assertive?

"OK, so I understand why being assertive is valid and that I'll feel better about myself. How do I do it?"

‣ There are basic techniques that you can begin to use immediately that will enable you to be more assertive. Changing your overall behavior will not occur overnight. It's an ongoing process with many little successes along the way. Coupled with the other approaches in this book, assertion will be a basic tool in your repertoire of time management skills.

Use "I" Statements

A basic technique in being assertive is the use of "I" messages. Particularly women in our culture have been socialized to be uncomfortable with using the word *I*. Somehow, that's been seen as an expression of self-centeredness—"If I'm always thinking and talking in terms of I, doesn't that mean that I'm selfish and only interested in me?" Actually, the use of "I" statements enables you to describe clearly and accurately what you're feeling, thinking, and wanting in an honest, straightforward way.

To shift from the use of "you" to "I" messages also requires a recognition that "you" statements often communicate a hostile, discounting message of aggression. For example, "You really make me angry! You've ruined my day" places the blame for what you're feeling onto the other person. In contrast, "I'm really angry! I feel as though my day's been ruined" is an acknowledgment of what *I'm* feeling. This is a more accurate reflection of reality. No one can *make* me angry, no one can *make* me experience my day as having been ruined. Even though the behaviors of other people and events beyond our control have an impact on us, we still choose our responses. At some level, I've chosen to feel angry and to believe that my day's been ruined. In using the "I" messages, a woman is acknowledging that those feelings and thoughts are hers.

In addition, the "I" statement is more likely to induce a positive response from the other person than is a "you" statement. You know how you may respond if someone is saying to you, "*You* did this . . . *you* did that." You're likely to respond in one of two ways: passively, by feeling insecure and intimidated, or aggressively, by feeling defensive and lashing back at the other person. Neither of those approaches is particularly conducive to good communication. "I" statements in which you're taking responsibility for your own feelings and actions will "invite" the other person to respond accordingly.

Notice too that the level of emotion being expressed with the "I" messages is as strong as with the "you" statements. "I'm *really* angry. I feel as though my day's been ruined!" In using the "I" messages, you can communicate your feelings and be in control of them. In other words, you can feel and think at the same time. You don't have to overwhelm yourself with your feelings, nor do you have to pretend they don't exist. You feel, you express your feelings, and you're in charge of them!

Short Responses Help!

Potential crisis situations in which tempers may flare can often be alleviated by the use of short responses in conversation. Our tendency in any dialogue in which some emotion is being felt is to talk on and on—each time it's our turn to say something. This will almost always lead us into either passive or aggressive behavior.

Janet may say to her co-worker in the plant, "Barbara, there's something I've been wanting to talk to you about.

Can we talk about it now?'' If Janet stopped there and gave Barbara the opportunity to respond, the initial statement would be assertive on her part. However, if Janet keeps talking, she's likely to become either passive or aggressive. Janet may end up saying, "Barbara, there's something that I've been wanting to talk to you about. Can we talk about it now? You know, I started to say something to you about three weeks ago . . . then decided not to. . . . Then, uh, I thought maybe I'd say something, oh, I guess, this morning . . . now, uh, I can kind of tell by the look on your face that you'd, uh, rather we not talk at all, uh . . . I'm sorry." Obviously, Janet, in continuing to talk, has literally talked herself into passive behavior. Not only her words but also her tone of voice and what she's communicating nonverbally will end up sending a weak, insecure message.

Another strong sign of her passivity is the "I'm sorry" tacked on at the end of her wandering comments. "I'm sorry," rather than being an apology for wrongdoing, is often a nervous response to fill an uncomfortable silence or even an overall apology for one's existence. If you find yourself saying "I'm sorry" many times a day, stop saying it—except in those situations in which you literally are apologizing for some statement or behavior on your part.

Keeping your responses short in conversations will also help you avoid becoming aggressive. If she's not careful, Janet in her conversation with Barbara may keep talking and end up saying: "Barbara, there's something that's been on my mind that I've wanted us to talk about. Can we talk about it now? You know, what you did a week ago is just like what you did three months ago. You're always fouling things up! You don't know what you're doing! You're incompetent!"

Obviously Janet has moved from assertiveness in her initial comments to aggressiveness as she kept talking. This could have been lessened or avoided altogether if Janet had

limited her initial statement to two sentences and given Barbara the opportunity to respond.

Both passive and aggressive behaviors waste time!
When you're passive, situations often remain unresolved,
continue to fester, and have to be dealt with time and
time again. Aggressive behavior generates tension and dis-
trust, which impede smooth and productive communication.
Assertive behavior enables you to deal with a situation at
the time in a direct and respectful manner. Assertion is a
timesaver!

Slow Down

Slowing down your rate of speaking will also help you to be
more assertive. The tendency is to speed up both speaking
and body movements when moving into either passive or
aggressive behavior. We get carried away with either the
emotions of passive insecurity and vulnerability or the defensiveness of aggression—the flow of our words speeds up,
our body movements become agitated! Slow down your rate
of speaking. Slow down your body movements. Even
though you may still be feeling upset and shaky internally,
by consciously easing your expressions externally, you'll be
communicating an assertive message to others and to yourself. As you do so, gradually you'll begin to calm down
within.

Deepen Your Voice

If your voice has the tendency to move into a higher register
as you feel emotions, deepen it. This will help you avoid
both passive and aggressive behaviors, each of which is
often characterized by a higher-pitched voice.

Monitor Your Tone of Voice

If you're communicating one message to someone with the
words you're saying and a different message with your tone

of voice, what will others hearing you always believe? Your tone of voice! It's the stronger message.

Experiment for a minute. Take the five words "Boss, I want a raise." First, repeat the words in a passive, insecure voice. Then, say the words in an aggressive, demanding manner. Finally, state the words in an assertive, firm voice. The words are identical—the tone of voice makes all the difference in the actual message that's communicated.

Regrettably, tone of voice is particularly difficult for us to hear in ourselves, although we pick up on it immediately in other people. How often we've said to someone, "It wasn't what you said, it was how you said it." You can probably recall times when you didn't even hear the words spoken by the other person because the tone of voice was communicating such a powerful message of its own.

It's important that you monitor your tone of voice so that you are communicating as accurate and congruent a message as you can. Mixed messages are difficult for anyone to understand and respond to. Two ways to be in charge of your tone of voice are:

1. Enlist the help of one or more persons with whom you have a close and trusting relationship. Ask them to give you periodic feedback as to whether you're communicating the kind of message they believe you want to communicate. They will hear nuances in your tone of voice of which you will not be aware.

2. Place a tape recorder on your desk or in your kitchen—any location in which there are a variety of conversations occurring in an hour or two. Turn on the tape recorder and let it record any conversations that occur. (Forget that the tape recorder is there!) Then, later, play back the recording and listen to your tone of voice.

In addition to discovering ways in which you need to modify your tone of voice, you'll also hear samples of excellent ways in which you use your tone of voice. It's as important that you be aware of the positive aspects of how you communicate as the negative. You can then be more intentional in building on the positive!

Important! Nonverbal Messages

What you communicate *nonverbally* is the most powerful message of all! Eye contact, posture, hairstyle, manner of dress . . . everything about you communicates a message—in addition to the words you're saying and your tone of voice. Although the exact percentages vary, a variety of research findings indicate that what you communicate nonverbally is often more powerful than the words you use and your tone of voice combined!

If Betsy is talking with her mother and is saying, "Of course, Mom, I don't mind if you stay with us another week," her mother will still get her real message of frustration and dismay by Betsy's furtive eye contact and her clenched jaw. How much better for both if Betsy would say to her mother in a direct, assertive way, "Mom, I've enjoyed your stay with us. Because of my schedule, it will work better for me if you do not stay another week now. Let's compare calendars to see when you might visit again." Perhaps not an easy statement to make, and there is the risk that Mom will respond in a hurt or angry way. However, the positive payoff will be there for Betsy: recognition that she's taken both her mother and herself into account. She expressed her feelings and wants without putting down or discounting her mother.

Mom, both consciously and subconsciously, will learn to trust and respect Betsy in a way she has not before. Also, Betsy will discover that she feels more congenial and loving toward Mom as a result of being straightforward with her.

Good nonverbal communication does include *eye contact*: not staring someone down and not always looking away—but, rather, naturally looking into someone's eyes for a few seconds, looking away, looking back, and so on.

Eye-level contact is an additional approach that will enable you to be more assertive. The situation: You're seated at a desk, someone walks over to you, and in this particular situation you want to be assertive about a specific matter. If possible, either stand up so that the two of you are more nearly on the same eye level, or invite the other person to sit down with you. Otherwise, if you remain seated and the other person is standing over you, psychologically it will be more difficult for you to be assertive.

There will be some situations in which it's inappropriate or impossible for you to get on the same eye level with the other person. If so, recognize that you'll need to increase your other assertive approaches to counteract the "one-down" setup.

Posture is a key to communicating assertively. If you're standing and want to be assertive, it's helpful to have your feet somewhat apart so that you're pulled into an upright, centered position. Not only will your posture be communicating a message of assertiveness to the other person, it will also be sending that message back to yourself. That's a far better stance than to stand, for example, with one leg twisted around the other. Then you're having to put some energy into keeping your balance, and you have less available with which to be assertive.

When you're seated and want to be assertive with someone, it will help to have both feet flat on the floor. Although this is not a comfortable position in which to sit for long periods of time, when assertion is needed, you will be presenting a centered and focused image both to yourself and to others.

Physical Appearance

Most people might agree that there is too much emphasis on physical appearance in our culture. Yet, as long as judgments are made about others on the basis of hairstyle and manner of dress, appearance will be a factor which contributes to or detracts from our assertive image.

To be assertive does *not* mean that you adopt a particular hairstyle or way of dressing. Rather, a part of being assertive is to take into account what your short- and long-range personal and professional goals are—*and* then to ask yourself whether your current personal appearance is contributing to your reaching your goals or is in some way blocking you from reaching one or more goals.

If blocks are there and you become aware of them, you can choose from one of three options: (1) modify whatever it is in your physical appearance that is a block, (2) modify one or more goals so that the former block is no longer relevant, or (3) do nothing. The element of assertion is that of going through a process of self-examination and decision making regarding your physical appearance. Whatever decision you then make is far more likely to be an appropriate and responsible one.

Again, the timesaving element of assertion becomes apparent. Trying to move ahead against one or more personal blocks is time-consuming and difficult. Removing any blocks enables you to move full speed ahead in reaching your goals—maximizing your potential and minimizing the time and effort required.

Assertion Attacks Timewasters!

TELEPHONE INTERRUPTIONS. An almost universal timewaster is *telephone interruptions*. Julie Jacobs has just begun to write her quarterly report when the telephone rings. She picks up the telephone, grits her teeth and halfheartedly responds to the person on the other end of the line—for twelve minutes! Finally, the other person winds down the conversation, the two say their good-byes, and Julie picks up her pen to start up again on her report. It takes her a few minutes to get back into her thinking and writing—then the phone rings again. She utters a cry of frustration, then picks up the phone. This time one of the people on her staff wants to discuss a meeting scheduled for later in the week. With a growing sense of frustration, Julie spends four minutes on this call before the staff member decides that he now has the information he wanted. After Julie hangs up the phone for the second time, it takes her even longer to focus her attention on the content of her report.

We've all been in Julie's shoes. You know the feelings of frustration, dismay, and finally resignation that come when the telephone interrupts your train of thought and your activities. Yet you may be allowing those interruptions to continue simply because you've not developed your assertive skills related to the telephone.

A major way to avoid many telephone interruptions is to screen your calls. If you are at an office and have a secretary, he or she should be trained to do that monitoring. If you don't have your own secretary, then often several people can pool their resources and share telephone answering. Even though you yourself may then be covering calls occasionally for others, you're still freeing up a greater proportion of your time.

If you have an office in your home or often do work at home requiring concentration, you have several options to avoid telephone interruptions: (1) have family members take messages for you, (2) employ an answering service, (3) purchase a message recorder, *and* (4) feel OK about taking the phone off the hook! Even thirty minutes of uninterrupted time can allow you to reap benefits in contrast to hearing that phone ring or anticipating its intrusion on your concentration. Remember, if it's important, the person will call again.

If you're in a situation in which you're obligated to take your calls, be assertive. Be sure to use "I" messages and short responses. Don't hesitate to say, "I'm not able to talk right now. May I call you later?" or, if the conversation has continued for some time, to say, "I need to finish our conversation now. I've enjoyed talking with you"—then one more sentence applying specifically to this conversation, such as "I'll call you tomorrow with the information you requested" or "Please let me know when you've located last year's statistics on the project."

Remember that your tone of voice on the telephone is the most powerful message of all. Listen to your own tone of voice to ensure that you're communicating an assertive message. A weak, uncertain, passive tone of voice can send a message to the other person that you can be manipulated and that you're likely to be weak in judgment.

In contrast, an aggressive tone of voice will communicate hostility and defensiveness, which will likely invite defensiveness back from the other person. An assertive tone of voice maximizes the influence and power of your message while still communicating empathy and respect for the other person.

DROP-IN VISITORS. With "drop-in" visitors, as with telephone calls, one of the best approaches is to have a screening process so that the potential drop-in visitor does not have immediate access to you. In an office, a secretary or receptionist can screen your visitors. Be sure the secretary has clear instructions on how to handle such situations, including how to set appointments for you or make referrals to other persons. The secretary can help you terminate your conversation with the visitor by calling you on the phone to indicate that a certain amount of time has elapsed. The secretary can also come to your door and indicate that other business needs to be transacted.

Another successful screening device is getting in the Quiet Hour habit. As described in Chapter 9, closing the door for at least an hour each day for reading, thinking, and planning is *not* a luxury. Rather, it is one of the most effective *time and stress* management approaches known. Use it!

When you do have visitors "drop in," you still have some assertive options to minimize the interruptions. As the person enters the room, you can say, "Hi, George, how are you doing? I've got only five minutes right now to talk." Or, if the person has dropped in to talk about something more substantive, you can say, "Helen, I know this is an important matter we need to discuss. My time is limited right now. How much time do you estimate we need to take on this matter?" Then, either schedule a meeting for later or agree on a time limit for this immediate discussion.

If the drop-in visitor persists in hanging around, continue your verbal assertive statements and also *stand up*. This is a strong, although not rude, signal that you are concluding the conversation. In those infrequent encounters in which the visitor becomes hostile, the same assertive approaches apply. Use the "I" language, slow down, and use short responses and a firm tone of voice.

INEFFECTIVE DELEGATION.   "It's easier to do it myself." "I don't know how to assign him that responsibility." "I don't want to make too many demands on others." These statements are typical of many women as they struggle to be more assertive in delegating. Women have been socialized to avoid placing demands on others. Many women have had far more experience in being the person delegated to, rather than the one doing the delegating. Consequently, for many women, it is an unfamiliar and disquieting experience!

When delegating, recognize that you have the right to ask for what you want, whether from family members,

friends, or co-workers. There's a myth in our culture that if
you have to ask for it, it doesn't count for as much. "If she
really cared, she'd . . ." "If he really loved me, he'd . . ."
It is an unrealistic expectation to have of anyone that he or
she is always willing and able to sense what our wants and
needs are—and to respond. How much healthier it is when
you assume responsibility and state what it is you want.
Why do you hesitate to do so? Because there is the risk of
rejection! The other person may say no. Granted, that risk is
always there—yet, that risk of rejection needs to be weighed
against what situation you're in right now because of *not*
speaking up.

As you take the risk of asking, you'll discover that your
success rate increases. You're getting what you want more
of the time. Developing the capacity to ask for what you
want has an immediate impact on your skills in delegating.
As you become more comfortable with your basic assertive
rights, you'll delegate more often and more appropriately.
For a more detailed examination of the benefits of delegation, its causes and solutions, see Chapter 8.

INABILITY TO SAY NO[1].   Maggie has difficulty saying no
to people, whether she's being asked to head up the next
major charity drive or to buy the new cleaning equipment
being promoted to her over the telephone. Consequently,
she's habitually giving away more of her time (and money)
than is appropriate or good for her.

Inability to say no is a major timewaster! It's particularly difficult for women to say no because of female socialization which urges women to always be supportive, caring,
and responsive to others (regardless of the personal costs).
Consequently, for a woman to say no necessitates making a
major shift in her own psyche.

[1] An analysis of the causes and solutions for the inability to say no is
outlined in Chapter 3.

It takes practice to be comfortable saying no. The first few times you take a deep breath and say no may be jarring, and yet you'll quickly realize that you are being more responsible to both yourself and the other person when you give such a response. Often, you can add to your no a brief explanation as to why you are declining. "No, I've already made as many commitments for this week as I can handle," or "I'm flattered that you've asked me to serve on the committee. However, my answer is 'No' at this time."

Keep reminding yourself that you have the right to say no and that in doing so, you are *not* being selfish or uncaring. You *are* being honest with and responsible to both yourself and others.

Assertive attitudes and behaviors will enable you to deal more effectively with every timewaster, whether it's attempting too much at once, unscheduled meetings, crises, socializing, or indecision. Remind yourself of your basic assertive rights and use the specific techniques of assertion in your encounters with others. Practice your assertion!

12

THE MANAGER/
SECRETARY TEAM

by Billie Sorensen[1]

We were wedded together on the basis of mutual work
and goals.

JUDY CHICAGO

The recent focus in training and development programs on
time management has had a direct impact on the perceived
role of secretaries. When a manager discovers the value of

---

[1] Co-author with Alec Mackenzie of "Time Management for Secretaries," a tape cassette program produced by Advanced Management Research.

142

time as an important resource, she realizes that to use that gift most effectively, the support of a professional secretary is invaluable. Many managers find that such assistance increases their own productivity 30 to 50 percent. And, as the secretary assumes greater responsibility, she is motivated to better manage her own time.

You have learned in previous chapters how time management principles including planning, organizing, and delegating are implemented individually. Here we will examine the role of the woman manager in working with her secretary, and learn how the secretary complements her manager, serves as liaison and ally to the management team, and works with multiple bosses.

The Manager's Role

Obviously the leader of the manager/secretary team must be the manager. She is responsible for making major decisions, determining top priorities, doing only what she cannot delegate. The effective manager will establish her secretary as a full-fledged member of her management team, as important to her as any other member.

Secretaries frequently bemoan the fact that they never have time scheduled with the boss to communicate and get answers to questions. If another manager walks in when the secretary and her manager are conferring, often the secretary must walk out, with unanswered questions. For this reason, the most important suggestion in implementing the team effort is this: *Devote the first five to fifteen minutes of your day (more if needed) to your secretary.* Keep that time inviolate. Use it to determine priorities for the day; to go over "to do" lists, written daily plans, and calendars; and to answer questions the secretary has saved for this communicating time. Your secretary should provide the files and other background materials you will need to complete the day's priorities.

During this time, you should delegate any tasks on your daily plan that can be done by your secretary. But delegation does not mean abdication. Weigh the suitability of the task against the capabilities of your secretary. If he or she is inexperienced, take time for training, recognizing that appropriate responsibility enhances growth. Analyze administrative operational duties as areas for possible delegation.

"Not kept informed" is one of the top five timewasters for secretaries worldwide. "Background" your secretary. If you are beginning a new project, give her the information necessary to answer questions and handle minor problems. "I don't know what the boss wants to accomplish, and I'm not sure how much responsibility and authority I have," laments the average secretary. Share your objectives with her and suggest that she develop a job description for your approval to clarify her own responsibilities with the authority to carry them out.

To preserve your own good image and save your secretary embarrassment, make it a habit when you leave the office to advise your secretary of approximately when you will return and, if possible, where you can be reached in case of an emergency. "You don't know where she is or when she will return? Are you sure you are really her secretary?" These questions were posed to a frustrated secretary by an irate client.

Keep the paperwork moving. Don't delay unnecessarily in reviewing drafts or decisions. Avoid perfectionism. Often the sixth draft of a report is no better than the second. Handwriting requires five times as long as dictating into a machine. By using a machine you can dictate at will without disturbing your secretary, and she can transcribe the tapes as schedule and priority require. If needed, obtain training on how to dictate and how to compose effective letters and reports. Let your secretary answer correspondence as her experience and ability permit, drafting replies for approval if your expertise is required. If you must handle some routine mail or read it for information, choose a time when priority work has been completed and you have less energy. Four in the afternoon is the hour many executives work on routine matters.

Use discipline to avoid interrupting your secretary unnecessarily. Jot down items to be discussed later if immediate response is not essential. She is trying to complete your priority work, which will be delayed by your interruptions. Give your secretary a quiet hour if needed. Establish a plan for controlling telephone and drop-in visitors. Once that plan has been agreed upon, give her the backup needed to carry it out. If you call out a word of welcome to the habitual drop-in visitor just as your secretary is turning him or her away, your secretary will be discouraged and unable to screen effectively.

"Credentialize" your secretary. Introduce her to your associates, clients, and customers. If her skills and abilities are excellent, advise your contacts that they should communicate their needs to your secretary when you are not available, knowing that she will handle problems effectively in your absence. This will conserve your time by eliminating routine and detail work.

Avoid asking your secretary to bring you coffee and to do personal errands. If she is truly a member of your management team, very likely she will volunteer, on occasion, since her motivation will be to conserve your time.

At regular intervals, review performance, discuss mutual problems and plans, and reinforce the team relationship. A meeting every three months for this purpose is a sound guideline to follow.

The Professional Secretary Complements Her or His Manager

A secretary's mission should be to help her manager achieve objectives most effectively, with the least expenditure of time, and to find a challenge of her own for job enrichment. In order to accomplish this, she must know the manager's long- and short-range objectives, keep current on organizational policies and procedures, and have spelled-out long-range objectives of her own.

One suggestion for a long-range objective is the development of a position job description with a manual of office operating procedures to accompany it. Our experience has been that not more than one in ten secretaries has such a job description. It can be used as a basis for planning and setting goals; it will confirm a secretary's responsibility and authority, and it will help her coordinate tasks with others. If a secretary is away on vacation or leaves her job, this information will provide a guide for the replacement. One secretary told us that she had recently taken a position where there had been no secretary for three months but because the previous secretary had left a thorough job description and an operating procedures folder, learning the new responsibilities had been greatly facilitated.

A professional secretary recognizes that scheduling time is not just setting appointments—it means looking at the day as a whole. It means setting aside time for the manager to work on her most important projects. Most secretaries estimate time requirements more realistically than do their managers and are more adept at running the calendar. Time logs will confirm the amount of time required for past projects and aid in setting a realistic schedule for the future.

"I wish my secretary would take more initiative" is the plea of most managers. Once a secretary has sufficient experience and is well informed, she should be able to discern the difference between the truly important and the merely urgent problems. She will handle the minor ones and know which should be referred to the manager. And, once agreement is reached on screening telephone calls and visitors, a secretary's good judgment and finesse are essential to avoid offending anyone.

Effective secretaries should try to arrange blocks of uninterrupted time for both their managers and themselves. A quiet hour to complete priority work should be available to secretaries as well as to managers. If a receptionist or other secretary cannot take over the phone, the manager may be able to answer her own for an hour.

A written daily plan with priorities and deadlines will organize a secretary's day. She may complain, "Why should I bother to set priorities when the boss will replace them with new priorities of her own by ten A.M.?" One good reason is that she will have a guide to return to once she has handled the manager's interruption. Otherwise, she may forget what she was working on and start a new task after each interruption. At the end of the day, she may have a number of tasks begun but none completed. The secretary will have less shifting of priorities if she shares her "to do" list or daily plan with her boss at the morning communicating session. It may be helpful to the manager if the secretary draws up a suggested list of priorities for her as well. Most managers appreciate this, and it permits the secretary to pass along reminders at the appropriate time.

A secretary shouldn't waste the manager's time. She should be well prepared for meetings, with lists of questions ready and background files and correspondence in hand.

She should be flexible, and patient, and she should remember that it can be more difficult to create a letter or report than to type it. Some revisions and retyping may be necessary.

A secretary needs to keep her sense of humor to ease the pressures of a busy day. If she makes a mistake, she should advise her manager so that corrective action can be taken immediately.

The Secretary as Liaison and Ally to the Manager's Team

A manager who tries to follow through on all details will not have time to manage, to think creatively. Undoubtedly, there will be stress from attempting too much and from lack of time for the really important matters. A professional secretary can serve as liaison—and ally—to the manager's team, checking progress on all projects and cooperating with team members in their efforts.

Often a manager is reluctant to delegate follow-up tasks to the secretary because team members have been accustomed to communicating only with the boss regarding their progress on a project. Lower-level managers sometimes feel rebuffed if they must deal with the secretary. In discussing the attempt of a secretary to obtain information for their mutual boss, one middle manager complained, "Why should I have to communicate through the secretary? My salary is three times hers—shouldn't the boss have time to listen to me?" A secretary, facing such resistance, may become frustrated, angry, and—finally—vindictive. When this happens, even more of the top manager's time may be required to cool tempers and heal wounded egos.

Such problems can be avoided if the head of the team communicates the reasons for delegating responsibility for follow-up to the secretary. The team must understand that (1) by working through the secretary they will usually get answers much faster than if they have to wait for the boss to get back to them, (2) this also conserves the boss's time for more important tasks, and (3) each team member will be given time with the boss when needed. It must be clear that the secretary is not attempting to build a wall around the boss, eliminating participative management by the team. A secretary must be sensitive to this issue and make an effort to correct any misunderstandings.

It is the responsibility of the secretary to act as ally to the team members, showing no favoritism. Each team member should be given uninterrupted time with the boss, when required. A weekly schedule of the team leader's time will help. Issued a week in advance, it accomplishes several things: (1) It shows what the boss is working on in case another manager has pertinent information to share; (2) It protects the secretary's time with the manager, since team members know she will schedule time for them as well; (3) It confirms appointments team members have made; and (4) It shows when time is available if an appointment is needed. If a request must be refused or delayed, the team member understands (See Figure 1 for sample schedule.) To ensure sufficient time for communication of team members with their boss, a period of "planned availability" is observed in

Figure 1

WEEKLY SCHEDULE OF M.A.R.

8:30–9:30 A.M. Quiet hour for department

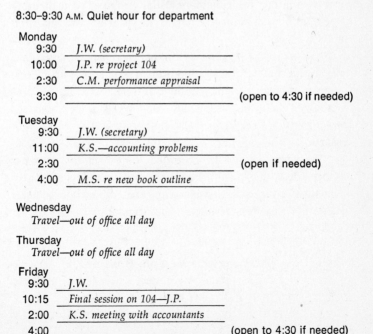

Monday	
9:30	J.W. *(secretary)*
10:00	J.P. *re project 104*
2:30	C.M. *performance appraisal*
3:30	(open to 4:30 if needed)

Tuesday	
9:30	J.W. *(secretary)*
11:00	K.S.—*accounting problems*
2:30	(open if needed)
4:00	M.S. *re new book outline*

Wednesday
Travel—out of office all day

Thursday
Travel—out of office all day

Friday	
9:30	J.W.
10:15	*Final session on 104—J.P.*
2:00	K.S. *meeting with accountants*
4:00	(open to 4:30 if needed)

some organizations. For example, the upper-level manager might select a time between two and three P.M. when she would be available each day for team members to phone or drop in (provided another team member was not in the office already).

A secretary performing a liaison role must be careful not to disappoint or embarrass the manager by misuse of the authority she has been given.

Initiative by the secretary will save time in meetings for all members of the team. Since meetings tend to fragment the day for many managers, control of time spent in this area is crucial. For all meetings, even between two people, the purpose should be identified and an agenda developed. Is this session for information, for reporting progress, for a decision? The agenda is then time-limited in relation to the importance of each subject. A time is set for ending. When time is limited, each member usually arrives at a meeting much better prepared. In Chapter 10, meetings are analyzed in detail.

When a secretary knows that her manager wishes to see the person requesting an appointment, she sets it up, determines with the visitor the amount of time necessary to complete the purpose and agenda, and advises her boss far enough in advance so that she can make any changes necessary.

Decisions should be recorded, dates set for progress reports, deadlines established for completion. The secretary then takes charge of the follow-up, keeping the team leader advised of any deviation from the original plan.

Working with Multiple Bosses

In today's offices, many secretaries work for multiple bosses—that is, two or more managers. Frequently a secretary supports as many as six or more managers. Communication is often nonexistent among the managers regarding the secretary's work, role, and relative priorities. She may find herself in the untenable position of trying to meet unrealistic deadlines for several managers at the same time.

The first step in working with multiple bosses is a meeting with all managers involved to reach agreement regarding how the secretary is to function. A secretary should not hesitate to take initiative in asking for such a meeting. Relative priorities on various categories of work should be established. Generally, on comparable priorities, the first work requested should be done first. When urgency or priority requires, the requesting manager should clear a shift in priority for the secretary with the manager whose work must be delayed.

Once agreement on relative priorities and procedures is obtained, a position job description with office operating procedures for the secretary should be developed and a copy distributed to each manager. Finally, one manager should be designated to determine which priority prevails in the event of a serious conflict.

A secretary working for only two managers should meet for five to fifteen minutes daily at a regular time with each, as we have suggested for the secretary/manager team. With three or more bosses, forms are extremely useful, since a daily meeting with each probably would not be feasible. Figure 2 is an example, but you should be creative in developing a form to serve the unique purposes of your job.

Where different managerial levels are involved, a secretary sometimes allocates a certain portion of the day or specific days of the week to work for each manager. While this can, at times, avoid dissension, it may not ensure that top priorities for the group are being accomplished. Allocation of time should be made on the basis of priorities. Don't wait until a crisis has developed to set up a plan for the work flow.

Figure 2

FORM FOR PAPERWORK FOR MULTIPLE MANAGERS

Subject: _____

Priority: _____

Deadline: _____

Discuss before typing: yes _____ no _____

Confidential: yes _____ no _____

Copies to:

_____

_____

Special instructions:

_____

_____

_____

A secretary can spend most of her day searching for multiple managers to answer phone calls and to deliver messages. The solution to this problem is to establish a message center on the secretary's desk, and require each manager to pick up her own messages. An "in–out" magnetic board will allow each manager to indicate absence from the office and the expected hour of return.

A log of telephone calls and visitors is helpful in any office. It is particularly useful for managers who travel a great deal. Usually, a few minutes spent reading the log will bring the manager up to date on events that have occurred in her absence. "Digesting" is another timesaver for the manager who makes long trips. The secretary opens and reads all mail, "digesting" the contents of each letter into a paragraph summary of the most important information. Several long letters usually can be summarized in a one-page digest. This digest is sent off to the boss, who replies by telephone or tape, telling the secretary what action should be taken. The practice of digesting will eliminate the stacked desk

Figure 3

TRAVEL ITINERARY FORM

Name: _____

Destination(s): _____

Date of departure: _____

Airline: _____ Flight: _____ Departing: _____ From (airport): _____

Seating preference: _____ Diet requirements: _____

Date of return: _____

Airline: _____ Flight: _____ Departing: _____ From (airport): _____

Seating preference: _____ Diet requirements: _____

Car rental: yes _____ no _____ Type of auto preferred: _____

Confirmed with: _____ From: _____ To: _____

Hotel: _____ Phone number: _____

Address: _____

Cash or traveler's check requirement: _____

problem which faces many managers returning after several weeks away from the office.

A travel itinerary form is particularly useful to a secretary of multiple bosses. Figure 3 is an example that should stimulate your thinking in developing the best travel itinerary form for your office.

Records Management

Because the amount of stored paper is proliferating and because the cost of locating lost or misplaced documents is escalating correspondingly, we have included in Figure 4 a chart of basic steps in filing. We recommend that a log be kept, for one month, of time spent in searching for lost or misplaced documents to determine whether your system needs attention. Our experience has been that most managers feel that improvement in this area is needed.

One final suggestion for working with multiple managers: Instead of distributing a copy of an informational

Figure 4

RECORDS MANAGEMENT

Basic Steps in Alphabetic Filing

Manager/Executive Secretary should:	*Secretary/File Clerk* should:
1. Place initials and date at top of sheet, indicating paper is ready to file.	Inspect letter or other paper to verify release for files.
2. Determine and underscore name or subject under which paper is to be filed. If subject is not on paper, write in at top of sheet and underscore.	Check paper for underscored words to determine where to file.
3. Consider using a code to save time in destruction or transfer of papers. Use code below, or adapt to your own requirements.	Be sure each person using files has copy of code system. Use code when transferring or destroying papers.

M—Destroy after 1 month
Y—Retain for current year
Y + 1—Retain for current year plus one
Y + 7—Retain for current year plus seven
UC—Retain until job is completed
P—Permanent

4. Index cross-references by determining and underscoring any words where cross-reference is desired. Place an X at end of line to identify cross-reference. If it is necessary to write in cross-reference words, do so. Underscore and place an X by these words also.	Make up cross-reference pages as necessary using colored sheets that are easily identifiable in files. Include on cross-reference sheet subject of paper, name under which it is filed, date of paper, and names of persons related to subject. (Numeric systems would require numbers of files.)
5.	Organize papers into alphabetical order to save time placing them in files. Place tops of sheets to left in folder. Put no more than 75 sheets in a folder.

Figure 4   (cont.)

6. Determine regular intervals such as every six months or once a year to clear out and transfer files.	Note transfer dates on calendar. Use code system to aid in transfer, retaining in current files permanent materials necessary for operation of organization at all times.

memo to each manager, the secretary should keep a central reading file with one copy of each memo in it. Each manager will be responsible for reading the folder once every two weeks to keep current. A secretary will keep the file up to date, discarding or filing material more than two weeks old.

Whether you are the manager or the secretary on your team, you rely upon and are responsible to each other. As a part of a well-functioning manager/secretary team, you will be maximizing your individual talents and also using your joint time and skills to produce effective results for your organization.

THE POSITIVE POWER OF A DEADLINE[1]

I've been on a calendar, but never on time.

MARILYN MONROE (1962)

The Deadline Is Tonight

"The deadline is tonight," said the accountant in measured tones, "tonight at midnight. If it doesn't show today's post-mark, it will be late and you'll have to pay a penalty." For many families filing their annual income tax return, that warning has a familiar ring. At some time, every head of a household in the country has considered the consequences of violating that deadline.

For some, it will be relatively meaningless. An executive chuckled, "Why, I've managed to mail my tax return on

[1] Adapted from "The Positive Power of a Deadline," by R. Alec Mackenzie and Deanna Scott, in press, 1980.

time only three times in my life . . . I'm not worried!"
However, a twenty-year-old, who was filing her first tax
return, had trouble collecting all the information needed.
She approached the deadline with visions of a jail sentence
and the concern of how she would ever be able to explain it
to her employer! But whether our response is lighthearted or
deadly serious, we all live most of our lives under the
shadow of deadlines of one kind or another. They come in
all shapes and sizes.

Under the Shadow . . .

For most of us, as children, deadlines and threats were indi-
visible. The school bell meant we had five minutes to get to
our seats. Term papers had to be in on time. We had to be
home by six for supper and have the car back by eleven. The
lawn had to be mowed on Saturday morning. With every
deadline, the threat of failure or loss of privilege was obvious.

Nick-of-time Experts

Getting things done on time . . . getting everything in on
time . . . getting to places on time. Most of us become
nick-of-time experts. Salespeople must deal with making
appointments and keeping them, turning in weekly quotas
and turning in quarterly reports, which will—sooner or
later—determine whether they keep their jobs. Nine-to-
fivers must arrive at work on time and face the constant
pressure of completing jobs on time, whether or not the
deadlines set by their bosses are reasonable.

Yes, the story of our lives is one of deadlines. At birth,
the doctor has only seconds in which to spank us into breathing. When we die, the funeral director will set a deadline
for the funeral. In between, for a lifetime, our sun rises and

sets, we eat and breathe, and each of us conducts the major activities of our lives under the shadow of deadlines.

Varying Views on Deadlines

Still, with all the pressures they impose, people react differently to deadlines. The executive took a lighthearted view of the tax deadline, realizing the worst that could happen would be a minor fine. Life is too short, he reasoned, to let deadlines dominate your life. On the other hand, the twenty-year-old was excessively anxious, believing that the government could do anything to her. These contrasting views toward deadlines reflect a deeper contrast in views toward time and life itself.

Attitudes on deadlines vary from the few who insist on always being early to those who can't make anything on time. Some plan their day to the minute, while others leave it entirely to chance, believing that spontaneity is essential in life. Some people set deadlines and religiously abide by them, punishing themselves if they fail to meet one deadline. Other people refuse to wear a wristwatch so that they have no reminder of the constraints of time. Some people consciously defy deadlines, equating the violation of deadlines with an autonomous statement of independence. William Emerson sought to demonstrate this last group with whimsy in his article "Punctuality Is the Thief of Time." Being late may have even saved his life. "There's no telling how many air crashes, train wrecks and shoot-outs I've missed by being late," he said.

Benefits of Deadlines . . . A Look at the Positive Side

Whether we honor them or ignore them, most of us never think of deadlines in a positive sense. Instead, we think of the relentless pressures they cause, the ascending stress that approaching deadlines exert on us, and the sense of frustration and failure we experience by missing deadlines. Let's examine some positive benefits of deadlines to help reverse our thinking. Deadlines can be viewed as a technique to enhance the management of our time and the quality of our lives as well as a means of actually reducing stress and tension at work and at home.

Deadlines force you to plan.

The "hidden agenda" in setting deadlines is the fact that you must think about what has to be done and how long it should take in order to set deadlines that are realistic. Your goals must be clear in order for you to determine the course of action to follow: to determine what you must do and when you must do it. Once the deadline is established for completion of a task, checkpoints can be set automatically for monitoring progress to ensure that you will meet the deadline. These steps—goals and objectives, priorities, deadlines and progress reports to ensure timely corrective action—are the heart of the planning process. Thus, setting deadlines becomes an essential tool in planning both your personal and work lives.

Announcing a deadline will help you get more done.

So long as the deadline we impose on ourselves is realistic, the pressure it represents can be positive and welcomed. By setting and announcing a realistic deadline for accomplishing something, we increase the likelihood of its getting done. The reason that this will work is that we are programmed from childhood to keep our promises. "Going public" by announcing a deadline is a promise to get something done by a certain time.

Deadlines help reduce stress.

Medical authorities have now related stress and tension directly to the two top killers, cancer and heart attacks, as well as to nervous breakdowns and a host of other physical ailments. The sense of anxiety and frustration generated by uncompleted tasks and missed deadlines can be eliminated by setting realistic deadlines and checkpoints. When progress lags it will be discovered at the next checkpoint so corrective action can be taken to ensure completion of the task on time. This assurance reduces the likelihood of crises and eliminates the worry, stress, and tension which almost always accompany missed deadlines.

Deadlines provide a sense of inner accomplishment.

By doing what you know should be done you're satisfying an inner need to be effective, to make a contribution, to perform up to your highest potential. Crossing out the most important item on your daily "to do" list can provide you with a deeply satisfying sense of accomplishment and of self-discipline.

Tips on Setting and Sticking to Deadlines

While deadlines are a powerful tool for getting more done in less time with less stress and tension, few women are as familiar with their use as they should be. Women juggling a career and home face twice as many deadlines as do many men and therefore need to be more familiar with their use and value. To make deadlines work for you instead of against you, here are some helpful tips:

1. List your goals and set priorities each day with deadlines for completing them. Use these deadlines to measure your progress and to say no to interruptions for less important matters.

2. Set your own deadlines when others don't. When receiving an assignment or a request ask the latest date it will be needed. Then set your own deadline with a realistic cushion to allow for the unexpected, and honor it.

3. Request deadlines on tasks given to others. Ask when your request can be met, then agree on a deadline. Be sure it is realistic.

4. Stick to a job until you finish. Do not permit interruptions except for more important matters. Recognize that interruptions are the most serious enemy of deadlines. When interruptions are unavoidable, return to the task immediately after the conclusion of the interruption. Remember, it takes three times as long to recover from most interruptions as it does to endure them.

Deadlines can be your friends—at home and at work—if you will only let them!

14

MANAGING YOUR HOME

Cleaning your house while your kids are still growing
is like shoveling the walk before it stops snowing.

PHYLLIS DILLER (1966)

The ultimate dilemma in time management for women? How can you efficiently and effectively manage your home and also pursue a career, further your education, and/or fulfill civic and cultural commitments? Your situation is further complicated when one or more children are at home. The demands are real and the expectations are high, both your own and also those of others.

Statistics back up the problems of the active woman in relationship to the management of her home. A recent study shows that working women end up with about ten hours less free time per week than either housewives or employed men. Statistically, not even household gadgets have given women an easy answer to coping with increased demands on their time. *The Use of Time,* a study written under the general editorship of Alexander Szalai, showed that the array of modern conveniences and technological timesavers made no difference in the amount of time spent on housework. The average woman in West Germany who has conveniences that might only be dreamed of in a small town in Yugoslavia got her work done in only one minute less per day than the Yugoslav housewife.[1]

When a woman goes to work or becomes involved in significant volunteer efforts, there usually is a tacit assumption that she will also still manage the home. She can delegate tasks to the rest of the family, but the burden of seeing to it that the household functions efficiently is usually left to her. Most husbands, who delegate to others at the office, willingly accept being delegated minor tasks at home. They are happy to pick up the loaf of bread on the way home but do not take the responsibility for checking the refrigerator to see what items are needed. One possible reason for this is that, in most cases, the wife's salary, if she is employed, is lower than her husband's so that they both feel her second job (outside the home) is less important than his. To compensate for bringing home less money, she has continued to assume the role of home manager, protecting her husband from unpleasant household details.

When a woman combines her role as a homemaker with a full-time commitment outside the home, she immediately doubles her need to be an effective manager! She is now managing two jobs; she must plan better and carry out those plans effectively.

To manage both a home and other commitments a woman must confront a variety of cultural attitudes imposed on her by others and also felt within herself. One of the most

[1] "Time Use Studies Reveal Plight of Working Women; Everyday Life in 12 Countries Has Common Design," ISR Newsletter, pp. 6–7.

powerful myths the woman must deal with is that of the Superwoman Syndrome—the notion that she must be all things to all people . . . and do it perfectly! A primary arena in which she is to express this perfection is her home. Regardless of the career and volunteer commitments she has, she may feel (and others around her may reinforce it) that she is to be a first-rate cook, a spotless housekeeper, a capable seamstress, an always loving and devoted wife and mother. A tough agenda for anyone!

Part of the problem in giving up the Superwoman Syndrome is that a woman, although under extreme time pressures, may still view her home as her "turf." Consequently, it may be difficult for her to relinquish control over what has traditionally been hers and even allow anyone else to help her.

In contrast, there are some women who go to the opposite extreme when it comes to managing their homes. Rather than feeling they need to have the "perfect" home, they do the opposite . . . and are notorious for having *the messiest* house on the block. Stephanie Winston suggests that extreme disorder in a home is psychologically "saying No to an authoritarian parent" and yet feeling guilty about it at the same time.[2] The standards of each woman vary. As one woman humorously commented when asked to name her timewasters at home, her top three were "irregular meal hours, sloppiness, and no place to hide." However, there is hope!

On a flight back from a week of seminars in Germany, one of the author's seat companions was the wife of an engineer in the Midwest. She had raised three children and for thirteen years had been a successful elementary school principal. In addition, she had developed a slide presentation called "Mission Impossible—the Role of the Elementary Principal." From time to time, she would visit state

[2] Stephanie Winston, *Getting Organized* (New York: Norton, 1978), p. 23

associations of teachers and school administrators to give her talks. With extensive use of delegation, planning, and minimizing such things as overhousecleaning and over-decorating, she managed her home as efficiently as she managed the school.

She had left her school without notice a few days earlier after receiving a call from Germany that her daughter was undergoing emergency surgery. When asked what kind of chaotic situation she would be returning to after four days of unplanned absence, she replied: "None at all—everyone knows whom to go to for decisions necessary to keep the school functioning." It seemed clear that she was a better principal than most and it was because of sheer necessity. She had decided she wanted to be both a successful homemaker and a successful principal and realized that this required planning and anticipating unexpected absences. Required authority was delegated in advance as part of her contingency plan.

Managing the home is a tough business. There is a budget to balance in the face of skyrocketing food prices. Family disagreements must be resolved, children chauffeured, pets fed, and on and on. Virtually all the management principles employed in the office have to be employed in the home at one time or another.

Timewasters at Home

The similarity between timewasters at work and at home is striking. When lists of timewasters prepared by middle-management supervisors and women reflecting on their use of time at home are compared, telephone interruptions, drop-in visitors, and crises are common to both. Other similarities include ineffective delegation, attempting too much, no daily planning, and failure to set goals and deadlines.

As evidenced from these comparisons and others, the telephone may be our best friend or worst enemy, either in

COMPOSITE TIMEWASTER PROFILE
(rankings by frequency)

TIMEWASTER	MIDDLE-MANAGEMENT SUPERVISORS	WOMEN
Telephone	(1)	2
Ineffective delegation	(1)	1
Drop-in visitors	3	9
Crisis management/Shifting priorities/Firefighting	4	6
Lack objectives, priorities, daily plan	5	5
Attempting too much	6	3
Cluttered desk/Personal disorganization	7	12
Meetings	8	17
Procrastination	9	8
Inability to say no	10	10
Chauffeuring children		4
Ineffective communication	11	24
Inadequate/untrained staff	12	13
Personnel with problems	(13)	
Incomplete information	(13)	
Leaving tasks unfinished	15	7

the office or at home. Husbands typically accuse their wives in an only semijesting fashion about being long-winded on the phone. Yet secretaries in our time management seminars list as one of their most common complaints of the male boss that he never gets off the telephone.

Shirley Belz of National Home Study Council is a strong advocate of staying *off* the telephone. Friends who stay on the phone with you for half an hour or longer often are using you as a substitute therapist. "Interject some of your own problems into the conversation," says Shirley, "and you'll soon find that they don't have time to talk."

In talking with women managers we find that they socialize, either on the phone or with drop-in visitors, less than other managers. They point out that they cannot take a briefcase home. They have a full-time job awaiting them after five o'clock and therefore must utilize their minutes in the office effectively. They are sometimes the brunt of caustic remarks from their male counterpart as they leave the office without briefcase. These men often feel that the woman manager is not carrying her share of the workload if she doesn't take work home.

The tendency to make unrealistic time estimates afflicts everyone, and the value of a daily written plan is quickly acknowledged by homemakers and office managers alike. Most housewives, for example, make lists of things to do, including shopping requirements. Getting things onto lists frees the mind for more important matters and also ensures against forgetting.

But a "to do" list does not solve the problem of planning the day and mapping out the hours so that one doesn't get sidetracked and procrastinate. As Shirley Belz commented: "I've noticed a typical friend who will start gathering laundry to take to the laundry room. When she is in the bathroom or kitchen supposedly gathering towels, she'll start cleaning the sink. The telephone rings. After hanging up, she goes on to the bedroom to pick up more clothes for the laundry. She decides the room needs vacuuming and starts that. Then it's time for coffee, after which she realizes she must fly to the grocery for butter before lunch, perhaps not even checking to see if other items are needed. And on and on. Consequently by noon, the laundry has not been done, other projects lie unfinished and she is exhausted."

Take a time log of your activities at home for a week. As suggested in Chapter 2, you'll then see how your time is being spent. A time log can be a tremendous aid in planning your time and delegating the work around the house.

Taking Time to Organize

APPOINTMENT BOOKS AND CALENDARS.   Just as it's important to keep an appointment book for career and volun-

teer activities away from home, it's also important to have
one place to record social and home-related activities. For
example, much time is wasted by keeping more than one
appointment book. It's not only a timewaster for you but
also an irritant to others when you say, "Oh, I don't know
whether I can play tennis next Saturday . . . I'll have to
check my *other* calendar." Note all your professional and
personal activities in the same appointment book, and take it
with you wherever you go.

One of the most effective and easiest-to-carry appointment books is the one which lists a week on each double-
page including an hourly schedule for each day. At the back
of the book is considerable space for listing most-used addresses and telephone numbers. It's a complete appointment
book and yet not too bulky for any size purse or briefcase.
In addition to keeping all activities scheduled in this way,
plus addresses and telephone numbers, you can paper-clip
together pages of the book up to the current week so that
when you open your appointment book, you'll immediately
have this week open to you. Finally, on the other side of the
paper clip (at the front of the book) you can tuck any actual
invitations or meeting notices so that you have additional
information about location or agenda readily available.

A DESK IS A MUST!   Even for women who are employed
and have a desk or even an office of their own at work,
there's still a need for a desk at home. It doesn't have to be
an elaborate one—in fact, it may not even appear to be a
desk to the casual observer (even a converted chest of
drawers or shelves in a closet can work). Some specific
location in the apartment or home is needed where the "business" of that home can be transacted.

In addition to the basic equipment and supplies needed
in any office environment, such as paper clips, rubber bands,
and stapler, have a telephone nearby if possible. It will save
much accumulated time over a month or year.

A simple filing system is needed in every home to keep all the legal and household-related documents in order and easy to locate. This will avoid the unnecessary frustration of never being able to find your policy number on the health insurance or locate last year's tax return.

In setting up the filing system, don't get too specific on choosing the title for each folder. It's better to start with general terms such as *taxes* and *insurance* and then get more specific as special categories emerge. Use typed labels if possible—they last longer and look better. If you keep any clippings at all, whether stock market reports or recipes, clip the first time you see them and file immediately. This will eliminate papers and magazines piling up or stray pieces of paper cluttering up your desk and your life!

One special file folder idea: Keep an accordion-pleated file folder with a separate section for each month of the year. Whenever you see a birthday card, have an idea about a gift, or any other idea you want to follow up on, even months ahead, buy the card or jot down the idea and file it in the appropriate month. Then develop the habit of checking the file at the beginning of each month. You'll have an immediate reminder of what special remembrances and activities you need to follow up on.

What about all those legal and household documents? What should you keep and where? The Bank of America suggests six categories of documents:

1. *Personal Documents:* These include key family records such as birth, marriage, and death certificates and should be kept permanently. Also included are passports, diplomas, and Social Security cards.

2. *Property Records:* Both real estate records (deeds, title papers, mortgage documents, and a record of capital improvements) and household inventory should be filed.

3. *Financial Records:* Needing safekeeping are any stocks and bonds, records for pension and profit-sharing plans, bank account information, and any retail credit and installment loan contracts.

4. *Insurance Records:* The policies may range from life and accident to liability and auto; keep any receipts and canceled checks.

5. *Tax Records:* Not only should you keep copies of your tax return forms, you also need to file all relevant receipts and canceled checks plus any other verification of your tax return.

6. *Health Records:* An up-to-date health record is an invaluable resource to have. This record should include such items as immunization records, infectious diseases, and any chronic symptoms or disease. To complete this medical record, get a copy of your dental record with perhaps even a current X-ray.[3]

Although most items can be kept at home, there are some that are best kept in a safe deposit box at a bank or savings institution. This will ensure safety from fire and theft of those items that would be difficult, if not impossible, to replace. The following list suggests what is best kept in a safe deposit box and what is appropriate for your at-home filing system.

Safe Deposit Box

1. Birth certificates
2. Citizenship papers
3. Marriage certificates
4. Adoption papers
5. Divorce decrees
6. Wills
7. Death certificates

[3] "Personal Record Keeping," Consumer Information Report #21 Prepared by Bank of America, Box 37128, San Francisco, California 94137.

8. Deeds
9. Titles to automobiles
10. Household inventory
11. Veteran's papers
12. Bonds and stock certificates
13. Important contracts

Active File (at home)

1. Tax receipts
2. Unpaid bills
3. Paid bill receipts
4. Current bank statements
5. Current canceled checks
6. Income tax working papers
7. Employment records
8. Health benefits information
9. Credit card information
10. Insurance policies
11. Copies of wills
12. Family health records
13. Appliance manuals and warranties
14. Receipts of items under warranty
15. Education information
16. Inventory of safe deposit box (and key)
17. Loan statements
18. Loan payment books
19. Receipts of expensive items not yet paid for[4]

PAYING THE BILLS. Though not a favorite job for most of us, paying the bills should be organized to be as painless as possible. Whenever you receive a bill, put it with the others—it usually will not need to be paid immediately. Once every two weeks or month, balance the checkbook and

[4] Excerpt from "Handbook for the Home," U.S. Department of Agriculture, 1973, prepared for distribution by the Consumer Information Center of the General Services Administration, Washington, D.C

prioritize bills to be paid (if all can't be paid at once). Retain
check stubs and canceled checks together in case they may
be needed later.

The Kitchen Is a Key to Effective Home Management!

The pivotal place for much activity in the home is the
kitchen. It's here that not only are the meals prepared and
often served, but also family members congregate infor-
mally with many decisions being made either leading to a
helter-skelter life-style or a more ordered, sharing-the-load
existence.

For the effective home manager, the kitchen is the best
spot for a family calendar. Ideally, the calendar is posted on
either the refrigerator or a bulletin board. It's here that each
family member posts his or her upcoming activities in addition to any family events shared by all. When conflicts in
scheduling develop, the kitchen is usually the setting where
compromises can be worked out.

Even though the kitchen is a focal point for family activities and often where visiting friends congregate, it is
primarily the place where food and food preparation equipment are stored and meals are prepared. Surprising amounts
of time and energy are wasted because the kitchen itself is
poorly organized. Canned food is stored on shelves in a
haphazard fashion; dishes, pots, and pans are scattered
hither and yon; and shelves may be overflowing with
appliances and containers that are rarely if ever used.

The woman who is concerned about managing her time
effectively must choose the kitchen as a primary target for
more efficient organization. The reorganization of the
kitchen shelf space is a key. For example, arranging the
canned foods on shelves according to the color of their contents is a surprisingly effective timesaver: all the green veg-

etables together (green beans, peas, spinach), the reds (beets and tomatoes), etc.

Even more important is the basic decision as to what supplies and equipment are actually needed in the kitchen. The only way to really know is to take all items out of the cabinets, look at them, decide what you use at all and then how much. What you haven't used for several months, either sell, throw away, or store in the basement. (If you don't use those items in the basement for a year, then get rid of them!) The items that are seldom used can be stored at the back of the kitchen cabinets, leaving room at the front for the more-often-used items. Also, get rid of any duplicate items; rarely do you need three sieves or four funnels to get you through an average week!

COOKING CUES. Buy food in quantity. Not only can you often save money in bulk purchases, you also cut down on the number of trips to the supermarket. Also, remember to never grocery-shop on an empty stomach! The macadamia nuts, the marinated artichokes, or the frozen German chocolate cake may seem irresistible in the store when you've not eaten for hours—but they wreak havoc on the weekly food budget!

Whenever possible in preparing meals, cook for several meals at once. Many dishes can be prepared and then frozen for later use. It's a good feeling to have worked hard all day and come home knowing that the meal is prepared, needing only to be popped into the oven.

Another great timesaver for women is a slowcooker. Food can be prepared the night before or early in the morning, the slow cooker plugged in before leaving, and the meal simmers all day while you're gone. Not only is the main dish planned and prepared, the aroma of the beef stew or chicken soup when you come home at the end of the day is a real boost!

The Challenge of Housecleaning

Few women enjoy cleaning house, and yet almost everyone reports that they feel better, with more control over their environment, when the housecleaning is done. You can take some of the frustration and drudgery out of your daily upkeep by following these pointers;

- Divide cleaning into segments. For example, take fifteen to twenty minutes each day on maintenance, with extra time devoted to your home or apartment one day a week.
- Start at one point in the room and work in concentric circles, rather than moving back and forth across the room—saves steps and time!
- Have all your cleaning materials in one box or pail so that you can move them easily from room to room.
- Use two clothes hampers, one for white and one for colored clothing.
- Do something pleasant while you're cleaning—listen to music or have a cake baking in the oven.
- Schedule your chores so that major tasks fall on days when your schedule away from home is lighter.

You Can Fix It Yourself!

A favorite myth about women is that they have no mechanical sense whatsoever. We've heard the comments: "Oh, she can't fix anything—she's a woman" "I don't know my left foot from my right when it comes to tools or how to use them."

The reverse is true. A growing number of women are learning home and car repair skills. The place to start is with a good toolbox. Judy Talley, a freelance writer and mother of two, has described the tools needed for a practical basic toolbox.[5]

[5] Judy Talley, "How to Get a Quick Fix-It," *Working Woman*, April 1979, pp. 65–67.

Her favorites include a *claw hammer*, preferably a curved-"claw" design, a *tack hammer* for the more delicate hammering jobs; a *nail set,* which looks like a pencil and enables a nail to be hammered into a surface while not damaging the surrounding area; *screwdrivers; pliers; saw; level; pipe wrenches; utility knife;* and a *tape measure*.

The toolbox (whether a carton, sack, or fishing-tackle box) also needs to include a variety of odds and ends. Judy suggests an assortment of "nails, nuts and bolts, wood screws, brads, tacks, sandpaper, pieces of wire, rags, and all those little leftovers from your various projects."

The tools themselves are important. In addition are needed a variety of glues, light machine oil, toothbrush, paintbrushes, and sealer.

Obviously, learning to use these tools and supplies will take time and patience. A basic "how to repair" manual can be a big help. Tackle each job as it comes along, and don't be afraid to ask the advice of another family member or friend . . . and *don't give up* if the first repair attempt fails. It's a matter of learning and perfecting your skills on a project-by-project basis. The saving in money and frustration will be well worth the effort. Good luck!

Managing Your Personal Needs at Home

GROOMING TIMESAVERS. Whatever your personal grooming habits may be, it's important that some routine be established, along with a single location for cosmetics and other supplies. Establishing a routine for grooming will guarantee that the basics are taken care of in addition to providing the optimal conditions for your looking your best. Many women report that their self-confidence and consequent effectiveness in their daily lives increases in direct proportion to how they perceive their own physical appearance. This is not to say that a woman should spend hours each day dawdling over her appearance. However, develop your own set of "how-to's" that are both time-effective and contribute to your positive self-image.

MANAGING YOUR WARDROBE. "Where's that belt I need for this dress?" "I thought I'd put that sweater in this drawer and now it's not here." "Oh, darn, I forgot a button was off this blouse!" It takes time and energy to face a disorganized closet and messy drawers each day! As one woman told us, "The hardest to find are things I put where they can't get lost."

A few hours or a day devoted to cleaning and organizing closets and chests of drawers can make a world of difference in how you feel about yourself in addition to saving time and enabling you to be more effective in your activities.

Even if your clothing space is limited, figure out some way to separate your clothes according to seasons of the year. Unless you live in a climate which is the same year round, you need to keep your summer and winter clothing separated, even if that means two different places on the same rod. Nothing is more frustrating than weeding through both wool skirts and sun dresses to try to find something to wear when the temperature is 65 degrees!

Plan what you're going to wear through the week. Then do any necessary mending and ironing all at the same time. You'll breeze through the week as a result!

An obvious how-to is keeping similar items stored together. Sweaters, slacks, shirts, blouses, dresses, suits . . . also belts. A good way to store belts is to hang all on a hanger at the side of a closet—easy to see and to pull off the particular belt you need.

The Big Question! How to Get the Rest of Your Family to Help at Home

How often have you thought or said, "What do I have to do to get some help around here?" Demand, plead, scream

. . . not particularly effective or pleasant approaches to use. And yet the reality is that many women are still expected to carry the major responsibilities in the home—even though they may have assumed other important commitments. To reeducate family members and gain additional assistance often takes time and patience. Perhaps the words of women themselves who have struggled with this issue provide some answers.

Involve family members in planning for the household. Enlist their participation in deciding on what chores are to be done and how to divide up that responsibility.

Author and lecturer Maggie Tripp offers some sage advice: "Women feel that if they don't go home at five o'clock and get the socks washed and the dinner cooked, they will lose their man. They are afraid to put the relationship to the test by confronting the issue.

"When women ask for help they begin to work out better relationships with the people they live with. Men are delighted to be included. It gets them involved in something helpful. Most marriages get perfunctory as they go along. This starts something positive in the relationship."

Biz Greene, an active careerwoman, wife, and mother of five, describes some changes she initiated when she started working full-time. "Each of the seven of us was responsible for planning and preparing one meal a week with automatic rotation of certain responsibilities. We also had a color-coded calendar with a different color for each person's entries—with red representing involvements of the entire family."

Biz also suggests that, when possible, you "Identify your values and needs and priorities (reassessing them from time to time as situations change). Then *communicate* them to each significant person in your life as you begin a time-consuming relationship (spouse, child, etc.), and reach an agreement on private time as well as shared time and responsibilities."

Maintaining an appropriate balance of freedom and discipline for children in the home is a valid part of effective time management. Another mother of a large family and associate professor of pediatrics, obstetrics, and gynecology at the University of Rochester Medical Center, Dr. Ruth A. Lawrence, comments, "I have always felt that my children's lives should not be totally molded because of my career. Although we have a large family, they are not regimented, and we are not raising each child in the same mold. They are encouraged to seek their own interests and to develop their own talents. I have never felt they should pay for my career by doing my work or carrying my responsibilities. On the other hand, however, I feel that any large family needs to work together, and the children do indeed have chores and responsibilities appropriate to their age. We do rotate jobs, and they occasionally get their choice, and when things don't get done that are assigned there are some restrictions imposed. I consider this part of discipline and training of any child whether his mother works or not."

A way to avoid undue fuss over scheduling problems is to have regular family meetings, perhaps a few minutes after dinner one night a week. This is the time to remind other family members of upcoming events and also to be sure that the calendar is updated with all necessary information. Family meetings are also a good time to agree on a shared work schedule for household cleanup, planning meals, and shopping. Depending on the size of the family and the availability of outside help, family members need to share the responsibility in maintaining a happy and healthy environment for themselves and each other.

Specific family-shared timesavers have been used successfully by Peggy Dolph, vice-president of marketing for a savings and loan association in Everett, Washington. For over thirty years, she's successfully handled her career and home. She suggests that in planning meals:

1. Make up a menu for the week. Let each person suggest his or her favorite dish—you'll get more variety.
2. Make up a grocery list from the menu so that all ingredients are on hand for each selection.
3. Select a convenient store to shop in, learn the layout, and make up your grocery list accordingly. This will really speed up your shopping and eliminate impulse buying.
4. Post the week's menu on the refrigerator door. The first one home starts dinner!

In enlisting the help of all the family, Peggy makes a list of all the recurring jobs: grocery shopping, putting the groceries away, preparing meals, cleaning up afterward, changing beds, washing, ironing, vacuuming, and so on. Let each person choose the jobs he or she is willing to do. (Giving them a choice works better than telling them what to do!)

Plan for large projects on weekends. Peggy suggests designating one weekend a month for a special work project. Make up a list to choose from and let the entire family have a voice in the choice. Your list could include:

1. Spring yard cleanup
2. Outside painting
3. Inside painting
4. Cleaning cupboards, closets
5. Garage cleanup
6. Baking for freezer
7. Canning
8. Repairs—indoor
9. Repairs—outdoor

Finally, make a list of weekend trips that would be possible to take because of a completed work project or a work weekend! Let everyone have a part in the selection—the payoff for a job well done!

Even though you may be learning to avoid many crises through better time management, there will still be those unexpected and unavoidable uproars at home. One young mother described her "moment of truth" as she struggled to cope with home, family, and the inevitable crises:

First I had to accept the fact that I am not an easy-going, sleep-in-the-dentist's-chair-person. Children's accidental food spills annoy me. Sudden shrill noises play tick-tack-toe up and down my spine. No mother can avoid these occupational hazards; but, I decided, any mother can make herself more shatterproof.

Since then, when a situation arises, I try to remember the saving formula STOP, LOOK, LISTEN—AND COUNT TO TEN. The day of the dog and clothespin incident, I stopped instead of grabbing the hairbrush. I looked and saw tears in my little boy's eyes. I listened and heard him sniffle, "Didn't mean to hurt Spot, Mommy!" And, as I counted to ten (figuratively), my reason asserted that our son hadn't been deliberately malicious—just curious, like any normal four-year-old.

Instead of an earthshaking scene, we had a calm be-kind-to-animals talk. We examined the clothespin and discovered how hard it could pinch. Then a contrite Mike held the box of tacks while I repaired the torn screen, letting off steam constructively with a hammer.

Unfortunately not all problems and solutions fit into a neat, quick pattern. Machines usually do what they are dialed to do; for example, the oven can ruin a cake at 550° when busy little fingers tamper with the range. (I've learned to keep a watchful eye on projects under way.)

There are plenty of places to pour bottled-up tension. While I polish silver to work off a black mood, my mind gradually ascends to more pleasant paths; the shine I put on our tea service is reflected in my spirits.

But household chores can themselves build up tension, can induce mental fatigue the same way homework affects a twelve-year-old. I reward myself at the finish line. For instance, I allow a half-hour to read when the ironing is done. Creative self-expression—painting, writing, music, knitting—helps counteract demanding routine.

. . . By cultivating calmness, I try to help our children build strength to cope. They'll need that, in a world already marked "highly explosive."[6]

It does take time and energy to respond to all the people and commitments in your life. You need a degree of self-understanding and love for yourself coupled with your nurturing feelings toward others. The struggle and the rewards are real. In her journal published in 1927, Katherine Mansfield said: "I want, by understanding myself, to understand others. I want to be all that I am capable of becoming. . . . This all sounds very strenuous and serious. But now that I have wrestled with it, it's no longer so. I feel happy—deep down. All is well."

[6] Mary Ann Gourley, "Listen to the Land" (Englewood Cliffs, N.J.: Countryside Press), p. 111.

15

"IN-BETWEEN" TIMES

The best time for planning a book is when you're doing
the dishes.

AGATHA CHRISTIE

How often women have commented to each other, "My
time is so fragmented! . . . If I only had longer periods of
uninterrupted time! Sometimes I feel as if I'm going off in a
thousand directions, never really accomplishing anything!"
Most women *do* experience their daily lives as fragmented,
juggling home responsibilities with career and community
activities: fixing breakfast while running a load of wash,
chauffeuring one or more children to piano lessons or
baseball practice, finishing up the project report, preparing a
casserole for the church supper, and packing for the out-of-
town regional meeting—a potpourri of activities and commitments that appear to leave little room for effective time
management.

But . . . the paradox is that it's often during these fragmented "in-between" times that you can tackle and complete a myriad of small and large projects which not only leave you with a feeling of accomplishment but also get a lot of jobs behind you.

For many women, working on these "in-between" tasks also provides a psychological boost to your own self-image. It's very satisfying to be able to experience both the more traditional aspects of your femininity through the tidying up of that recipe file or the completion of a letter to that favorite relative, along with the more important parts of your daily activities such as completing the flow chart that's due in the office tomorrow or writing the committee report that will finalize the agency's pending strategy for the year. There's a kind of internal harmony you'll feel as you make your in-between times work for you—in all aspects of your life.

When do these in-between times occur? The first step in making these periods time-effective is to be aware of when and where they exist. This can best be determined through relying on a time log or daily journal to keep you posted on how you're actually spending your time each day.

Jean Bradford encourages us all to become "wait-watchers"; monitor yourself and recognize those times when you're waiting and doing nothing.[1] Commuting, waiting for appointments, a session at the beauty parlor, even traffic jams are all times when you can do more than just sit and fret. The timesaving activities possible at these and similar times are far-ranging.

To make use of in-between times, you must have the material and supplies you need readily at hand. The most important of these resources is often a briefcase.

---

[1] Jean Bradford, "Getting the Most Out of Odd Moments," *Reader's Digest*, June 1971, p. 82.

You and Your Briefcase

As women enter the world outside their homes, the use of a briefcase becomes an interesting issue. Do you need one at all? If so, what kind? Should you carry both a purse and briefcase?

When practicable, carry one good-looking bag which can double as a purse and a briefcase. It looks better than struggling to manage two slippery bags (especially in revolving doors!) and gives a more executive image. If possible pick a neutral color which can be used in at least three seasons, with different-colored clothing ensembles, so you don't have to be changing it periodically.

There are timesaving approaches to organizing briefcases—a briefcase filing system. Color-coded file folders are helpful, or use tabs to identify categories. Depending on the specific nature of the work you do, you can categorize your briefcase contents and consequently not always be searching for that one letter or notation misplaced among the other items.

A woman judge we know has file folders in her briefcase with the following designations: Phone Calls, Read, Type, Handwritten, and Office. When she receives her phone messages at her office, checks her answering service, or receives a memo asking for a telephone response, she will, if possible, return the calls immediately. If that's not feasible, she puts those messages in the Phone Calls folder to be made as soon as convenient. The same is true for the other categories. The Read file is for reports, newsletters, briefs, etc., that she wants to read as soon as time allows; the Handwritten file is for all personal notes she plans to write; and the Type file contains all correspondence, first drafts, etc., she needs to type herself. The Office file is for any items of business that need to be dealt with one-on-one in the office, including conferences, putting items in the files, or directions to her secretary or other staff members regarding upcoming events.

The value of this briefcase filing system is that it keeps material organized and easy to retrieve. With her briefcase as a resource, a saleswoman waiting for appointments can use that time to write reports or think through her presentation. If the location and time are conducive to twenty minutes near a phone, she can pull that file and move through several calls quickly. If she's waiting for a doctor's appointment, she can quickly pull the Read file and skim or read several items in the waiting room. (Barbara Walters, television news personality, told the authors she reads "everywhere, all the time.")

The woman who uses the system described above reports that if she has two hours of work time available, she will sometimes tackle the Handwritten file first because that's what she's most in the mood to do. At other times it may be the Type file. Thus, another benefit of using this briefcase filing process is that she is able to make maximum use of blocks of time matched to her energy levels.

Another woman we know who makes effective use of her in-between times is Ann Richards, County Commissioner in Travis County, Texas. She describes her organization of working materials as follows:

We use a system of color-coded folders, though "system" may be too kind a word for it. The notion is that critical things are in red folders, while Court and Worksession materials are in orange, "can wait" reading is in green and speeches or meeting materials are in blue folders . . . I make good use now of postcards for brief notes, and try to handwrite most letters of a significant nature that are neither long nor technical. With other letters or anything else requiring action I put a note indicating what I want said or done into my Aide's box which is on my desk.

A "Carryall"

If a briefcase is inconvenient or inappropriate, an option is a carryall bag—large enough to have two or more compartments and bulky enough to hold small items of clothing or a book if necessary. Whether you're waiting for your medical appointment or waiting in an airline terminal for your next flight, a carryall can enable the following options: mending small items, reading and making notes on tomorrow's agenda, writing a few thank-you notes, jotting down gift ideas you'd forget otherwise, brushing up on your French or Spanish with a handy language guide, or even refurbishing an out-of-date recipe file. As described in an earlier chapter, in-between times are also ideal for compiling "to do" lists for the next day or week.

Doing Two Things at Once

Often time can be conserved by literally doing two things at once. This can equal up to ten hours of extra productive time each week! For example, a great timesaver for many women is to have an unusually long cord installed on the kitchen telephone. Many a thoughtful personal or professional discussion has ensued while the woman is preparing a meal, cleaning up the kitchen, or putting away the groceries. Obviously, it's important to check with the person at the other end of the line as to whether your activity will bother him or her. If the other person gives the OK, then "full steam ahead." Rather than distracting you from the substance of the telephone conversation, your activity in the kitchen, which usually is routine in nature, enables you to concentrate more fully because you're being effective in two jobs at once . . . you focus in!

Other examples of "doubling up" include signing your daily standardized letters while your secretary briefs you on tomorrow's schedule, repairing your fingernails while talking on the phone, chatting with your children as you prepare the evening meal together . . . and if you're a suntan addict and have some flexibility in your work schedule, have a phone jack installed on your porch or in your backyard. Sneak a couple of hours on sunny days, grab a lounge chair, plug in the telephone, and get caught up on your phone calls. Conferences have been planned, charity funds have been solicited, and floundering projects have been rejuvenated while at least one of the persons in the conversation has been soaking up the sun!

Carrying a small tape recorder with you can be very helpful. Whether driving the car, waiting for the bus, or sitting in an airline terminal, you can quickly record any messages or the "germ of an idea" that might be missed otherwise. If you're attending school or a training session, it's a great help to have the tape recorder handy to record part or all of the lectures or at least to record key points immediately after the session.

Doing two things at once also includes exercise! Some relaxation exercises are suitable for those few minutes in a traffic jam or while cooking dinner. More extensive exercising is possible when watching television, whether the morning news or while catching your favorite prime-time show in the evening. Many bright ideas have come during showering or jogging times. The head of a New England university department of English keeps a "think-about" list of subjects to mull over in her mind during such non-thinking times as the weekly shopping trip.

Time for Doing Nothing

Our time *should not always* be filled with activities! A healthy and productive woman knows that she must allow time for doing nothing, to let go of the frantic pace. We each need to monitor ourselves closely so that we know when to slow down or stop, rather than filling even our in-between times with more hustle and bustle! Here is a marvelous statement in support of the occasional do-nothing time:

WHITE SPACE

White space is what we editors call the area on our pages not taken up by type and pictures—it sets off what we have to say, just as space sets off the branches of a tree.

Empty space in your house will do the same for you. Every room needs some breathing space, free from pictures or patterns or objects. These restful areas of nothingness set off the things you do want your family and friends to see and enjoy.

Each day needs some "white space" as well—some mental breathing space, to set off the activity and give it meaning.[2]

Saving Time While Traveling

Planning Your Trip

A key to successful travel is planning. Some stress is involved in any movement from one environment to another, and planning will do more to lessen that stress than anything else.

A key element in planning your travel is to clearly identify the purpose of each trip. But why? Surely you know why you're going to take a trip—it's a vacation or a business trip or maybe a combination of both. Isn't that enough to know? In most cases, it is not! . . . *if* you're interested in productively planning for your trips.

Alternatives to Making That Trip

Any business-related travel needs to be closely evaluated to determine whether it's really necessary. Are there other alternatives that would be more economical and effective? Consider:

1. Could you conduct the business by phone, either with one person or through a series of conference calls? This alternative is far more economical and in some cases can be as effective as a long-distance trip.

---

[2] Gertrude Dieken, "Listen to the Land," (Englewood Cliffs, N.J.: Countryside Press). p. 115.

2. Can you write to the other persons with whom you were otherwise planning to meet? This might be accomplished in letter form, a project report, or even by one or more cassette tapes.

3. Could the trip be postponed? There is always the question to ask: Might this trip be more effective later in the year, when we have more information on the project evaluation or when the new agency executive has had a few more months to implement her management plan?

4. Can this trip be combined with others? If you're planning a trip to Boston in late April and need to meet with someone in New York before June first, it is obviously a time-and-money saver to combine the two trips into one.

5. Does it make more sense to bring the meeting to you? It may be that the key persons you're planning to meet with will be in your area within three weeks. You can arrange to meet with them while they're near and transact any additional business with their colleagues by phone.

6. Is there someone else in your company or agency who already has a trip scheduled to your destination and could transact your business for you? It's obviously a waste of time and money for both of you to make a trip when one could handle both transactions.

Travel Timewasters

The typical business traveler wastes more time on trips than when in the office. The following oversights tell only part of the travel story for most:

1. Not "managing your absence" by preplanning with associates and subordinates what actions will be taken in your absence.

2. Not thinking through primary *and* secondary objectives which might well be achieved at the same time.

3. Not planning far enough ahead to ensure that plans of others can be coordinated with yours, nor in sufficient detail to ensure optimum utilization of your own time.
4. Not planning the most advantageous schedule and the best use of time en route; i.e., to think, plan, read, listen to tapes, write, or dictate.
5. Not summarizing results or conclusions, and not preparing initiating or follow-up actions *before* return to office. (Do this as soon after the conference as possible, before details slip from your mind.)

While some timewasters are peculiar to travel time, many are identical with those occurring back home. An effective time log will show the ones with which you have trouble.

"Take With" List and Briefcase Preparation

For trips that will involve a meeting or series of meetings covering a number of subjects, a "take with" list of everything you will need to have available for various discussions is a great help. It should be started well ahead of the trip so that as items come to mind they can simply be added to the list.

Before Mary Kay Ash leaves on a trip, her assistant prepares a folder containing complete information for each hour and day of that trip, including phone numbers of key contact persons. She attaches to the front of the folder the travel itinerary with time, flight, etc.

There will likely be projects or tasks to be thought about, memos to be written, correspondence to be answered en route. Trips by air provide a unique opportunity for concentration without interruptions from four of the top timewasters worldwide: no telephone calls, no drop-in visitors, no meetings—and, we hope, no crises. With that level of insulation from the normal hazards of the working environment, a well-prepared manager can get three hours of work done in one hour of flying time. This single fact should persuade cost-effective managers as well as their controllers that first-class or business coach travel, if well used, could easily pay for itself many times over because of the work that can more easily be accomplished in the air than in the office.

By all means have those papers on which you intend to work in your briefcase for easy access along with your portable dictation equipment or writing materials. Many travelers listen to tapes while riding in automobiles, thus accomplishing educational and self-development objectives while commuting to work or traveling on assignments. Telephone calls can be made at the airport while waiting for your flight connection. Whether you use public transportation (where reading, writing, dictating, or discussing problems are possible) or whether you drive (which permits thinking, planning, tape-listening, and—in special situations—dictation), effective managers utilize travel time for many varied and vital purposes.

Packing Tips

The biggest hassle for many women in traveling is packing—either taking too much, not enough, or too many of the wrong items. Here are some travel tips for today's woman which can relieve the strain of any upcoming trip:

WHAT TO TAKE

Permanent press clothing

Loosely woven fabrics

Basic dresses—coordinated colors

Only a few pieces of lingerie needed—can wash out overnight

Keep extra cosmetic bag always packed (include toothbrush, toothpaste, aspirins, makeup, small sewing kit, mouthwash, first aid items, detergent)

A compact or disposable raincoat to carry in baggage or purse

PACKING

Use smaller pieces of luggage rather than one big one

Place each clothing ensemble on hanger in separate full-length plastic bag (ready to put in closet when you unpack)

Pack clothing tightly—will lessen likelihood of wrinkling

Pack purses and shoes in individual plastic bags (provides them protection and also keeps rest of suitcase tidy)

Pack all "have-to" items in carry-on luggage so that in case your other luggage is late in arriving, you have what you need to get through the day or night

Pack smaller clothing items such as blouses and scarves in tissue paper to prevent wrinkling.

Use a shoe bag (Six or more pockets) to pack hose, hair dryer, belts, etc. (when unpacking, just unfold and hang in closet or bathroom)

Place name and address tag *inside* each bag in addition to outside identification (in case outside tag is lost)

UNPACKING

If your clothing is wrinkled, put on hangers in bathroom, close door, and turn on hot water to create steam room—most wrinkles will disappear

Unpack and "settle in" your hotel or guest room as soon as possible after arrival. Create as neat and homey an atmosphere as you can—it helps you to feel secure and in charge of your environment!

RECORD-KEEPING

Keep expense records on a daily basis

Use a full-size envelope in your purse or briefcase each day to store receipts from hotel, meals, taxis, etc.

When charging any expenses, use the same major credit card. Ideally, use that credit card for your travel charges only.

Travel time and in-between times, in general, provide additional opportunities to be time-effective. Monitor yourself and recognize those opportunities as they present themselves. You won't regret it.

16

LETTING GO
OF STRESS

One by one the sands are flowing
One by one the moments fall;
Some are coming, some are going;
Do not strive to grasp them all.

ADELAIDE PROCTOR (1869)

"Sometimes I feel like I'm going to explode!" . . . "The
minute I walk into that monthly meeting, I get a headache"
. . . "He calls, I get a knot in my stomach!" How many
times a day or a week do you make similar comments?
Women today are leading such hectic lives that they are
finding not only fulfillment but also heightened stress and
anxiety. Improved time management can lessen stress!

The causes of stress in today's women vary, ranging
from the Superwoman mentality with its unrealistic self-
expectations to being the lone woman in a visible position of
responsibility. Increasing numbers of women are becoming

workaholics, addicted to their work not only during the week but also on evenings and weekends. The neurotic drive to "be perfect" often propels a woman into too many commitments and "spreading herself too thin." Women also tend to "sandbag" their anger, collecting hostile feelings inside rather than expressing them in safe and appropriate ways. Stress also will result from a woman's tendency to strive for efficiency and exemplary detail work, neglecting the often more important process of conceptualization.

At a psychological level, women will even create their own stress by being too busy with too many responsibilities in order to avoid intimacy with others. A woman may use a hectic life-style full of commitments and activities as a way to protect herself from meaningful relationships, thus avoiding the risks of self-disclosure and possible rejection. Stress and tension will result from this avoidance.

External factors also contribute to a stressful environment for women. Family members or friends may have unrealistic expectations of a woman, wanting her to have the "perfect household," the "best children," *and* the highest bowling average on the block. In the work setting, a woman may encounter sexist remarks, discriminatory practices, and/or the pressures of being the token woman who makes or breaks opportunities for other women in the organization depending on her performance.

Women *are* living in an era of rising expectations, the pressures of which can result in stress symptoms of exhaustion, ulcers, heart disease, high blood pressure . . . the list goes on and on.

Is it possible to have an active life-style and still manage stress effectively? Yes—and time management provides a key. If you can learn to identify your stress symptoms, understand at least to some degree the causes, and then modify your attitudes and behaviors, the stress symptoms will lessen, and you will have profited both physically and emotionally.

What Is Stress?

Stress is a reaction to perceived events, usually physiological in nature, experienced in response not only to negative events but also to pleasurable occurrences. We experience stress when falling in love as well as when facing a serious illness.

Although stress is a universal experience, we each have developed our own unique symptoms of stress, the weak links in our own systems. Janet Lock in charge of a computer department may develop a headache several times a week, while Dolores Johnson may get a chronic uneasy feeling in the pit of her stomach. In a very real sense, we each generate our own stress symptoms.

I Choose My Stress!

One helpful exercise in dealing with stress is to think of the symptom as not being foreign to your system, not something external that's being imposed on you—but, rather, a condition that you're generating yourself. The more you can "own" your own stress, the more understanding and control of it you can develop: *my* headache, *my* tense stomach, *my* shaky hands.

The more you recognize that you create your own stress symptoms, the more able you are to answer the questions, "Why am I giving myself this symptom?" "Why am I generating a headache for myself?" "Why am I tensing my neck muscles?" Often by asking questions in this manner, you'll have an immediate insight into the cause of the stress and then can begin a problem-solving process of dealing with the cause.

Stress and Time Management: Are They Related?

How is the reduction of stress tied to effective time management? The relationship is clear. One of the most common

reasons given for heightened stress is "not enough time"—
and more often than not, not having enough time is a direct
result of poor time management! The issue is *not* how to get
rid of the stress but, rather, learning how to manage stress
effectively.

In addition to all the time management approaches described throughout this book, there are some that are particularly relevant to stress reduction. With special attention to
these, a woman can begin immediately to lessen the tension
in her life.

Organize Yourself

Organizing yourself is a key—the best first step in reducing
tension related to "not enough time." Set aside a day or
more if necessary to do nothing but reflect on your current
life, the activities and people involved, and sort out your
priorities. Then set both short- and long-range goals related
to those priorities.

Keep a Daily Journal

Writing down not only the events of the day but also your
feelings about those events does two things. It provides you
a visual symbol of how you managed your time that day, and
it also provides you a way to get your feelings out, to debrief
your emotions, and gives you a more objective perspective
on your reactions to situations. You can monitor both the use
of your time and also what situations trigger stress in you.
Through this increased self-understanding, you're able to be
more in charge of not only your time itself but also your
emotional reactions.

Set Aside Time for Relaxation

A growing body of research indicates that the ability to relax
is a key to a long and productive life. And time to relax can
range from a five-minute relaxation exercise to a full day of
"roaming." A physical break over lunch such as a walk,

bike ride, or swim is highly recommended because of its restorative value.

All of us feel occasional stress almost every day—a few minutes or a few hours at a time. Two to five minutes of relaxation exercises at those times can reduce the impending headache, the tightness in your chest, or the ache in your neck. One favorite of many women is to consciously slow down their breathing and also take deeper breaths, slowly counting to ten.

Rosalind Forbes suggests further in *Corporate Stress* that each time you think or say the word *I*, you inhale. As you exhale, say the word *am*.[1] Another approach is to tightly clench the muscles in your face, hands, feet, all over your body for ten seconds, then release and relax . . . tighten . . . relax . . . tighten . . . relax.

A related relaxation approach, as you breathe more slowly and deeply, is to imagine yourself being in a serene and safe setting someplace in the world: a mountaintop, on the beach—any place where you are alone and secure. Even a few minutes of fantasizing yourself in that environment is relaxing. Many women report the tension easing away quickly.

Be "In Training" for Your Life-style

Just as an athlete trains for the big event, you can develop a training mentality to manage your busy life-style. A friend recently described how she reacted upon discovering that her blood pressure had gone up and that she had some early signs of heart disease. Although the doctor had not prescribed any medication or treatment, our friend knew that she didn't want the symptoms to continue. Being a happily active woman with many personal and professional com-

---

[1] Rosalind Forbes, *Corporate Stress* (Garden City, N.Y.: Doubleday, 1979), pp. 170 ff.

mitments, she took a serious look at her current life-style and considered modifying it—perhaps eliminating one or more activities, curtailing the remainder. Immediately, she realized that she loved her current life and didn't want to make any major modifications. She then began to think about what she could do to get herself in optimum shape, physically and mentally—as if she were literally in training for a major athletic event.

She was encouraged in this approach by recent research indicating a direct link between sound nutrition and exercise and lower blood pressure, less heart disease, and overall better health. She's now developed for herself a regular routine of walking at least forty-five minutes each day along with some newly developed eating habits which include less fats, sugar, salt, and liquor (and no cigarettes!) and more fruits, vegetables, and carbohydrates. The blood pressure is lowering, the early symptoms of heart disease are dissipating, and she feels terrific! The life-style she loves is intact, and she's now in peak shape to meet its challenges!

Match Your Tasks to Your Energy Level

Matching your tasks to your energy level is highly recommended for reducing stress. Schedule routine tasks like correspondence or returning phone calls for low-energy times, while targeting top-priority and most demanding tasks for your highest-energy times. Most people are early starters, meaning they are at peak energy levels early in the morning and tend to run out of steam toward the end of the day. However, most of us put off the more important and difficult jobs, preferring to start on the less important tasks because they are easier. The consequence of this behavior is shown on the graph in Figure 1, on which are plotted our typically decreasing energy levels against increasing task demands. The shaded portion below both lines represents the effectiveness of results achieved.

The end result of matching tasks to energy levels is evident on the graph in Figure 2, where difficult jobs are scheduled first instead of last, and the low-value tasks and routine details are scheduled at the time that energy level is lowest. Here the shaded portion under both lines is now approximately doubled, indicating a great increase in overall effectiveness.

Describing how she matches her energy levels to her tasks, Shirl Brenneke, a freelance journalist, wife, and mother, says, "Learn your own creative best hours and seize them for your most important writing or problem solving. Mine comes as early as four-thirty A.M., when I become

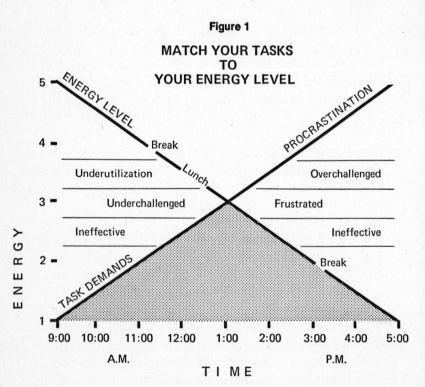

Figure 1

**MATCH YOUR TASKS
TO
YOUR ENERGY LEVEL**

'awake behind my closed eyelids' and *want* to get up and get to my typewriter. No one phones at that hour to interrupt my flow, and it's great to get a two-hour jump on the day."

Dr. Eleanor Schwartz, Dean of the School of Administration at the University of Missouri at Kansas City, prolific author and lecturer, mother and homemaker, agrees. "I write almost every morning between five and seven A.M.," says Schwartz. "I find these hours the most productive because I'm fresh, alert and at my creative best. And, of course, there are no interruptions. The rest of my day is rarely my own. The demands of administrators, faculty, students and publishers as well as the business community

Figure 2

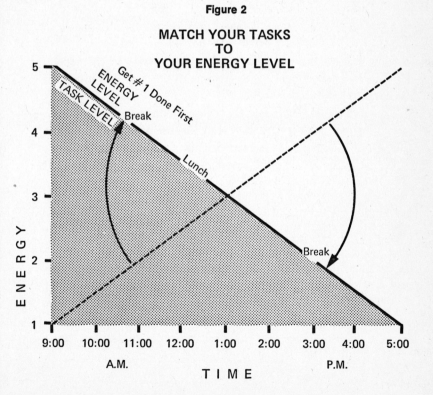

**MATCH YOUR TASKS
TO
YOUR ENERGY LEVEL**

never end. I've come to prize those early morning hours most highly. This is *my* time!"

Accept Change

Change is an inevitable part of living. However, we don't always welcome it with open arms. In fact, most of the time we resist change, even when we know that the current relationship or situation we're in is not good for us. At least it's familiar, and there's a kind of security in that. As we contemplate a change in that relationship or situation, the fears set in. Often they are unrealistic fears, sometimes approaching even catastrophic expectations.

Rather than allowing unreasonable fears to take hold of you, ask yourself, "What's the worst thing that could happen if . . .?" and "Could I cope with that if I had to?" Almost always, the answer to the first question is not nearly as bad as the initial fear, while the answer to the second question is almost always affirmative: "Yes, I can cope if . . . ."

Embrace change. The more you are able to do so, the *less time* you will spend in lamenting the past and fearing the future. You will be psychologically freed to make the most of the present. You'll be operating at a maximum level of efficiency and effectiveness.

Create an Attractive Environment for Yourself

A cluttered, dirty, or drab environment contributes to stress. We're all affected by our physical surroundings, and the appearance of our home or office can have a positive or negative impact.

Take a few minutes each morning to tidy up your apartment or home. Many women report that getting up fifteen minutes early each morning to do so is well worth it for the feeling of satisfaction that results. An additional payoff is that it gives us a feeling of *control* over our environment. All of us as humans have a desire to be in control, to be in charge. Often this need is acted out in destructive ways in relationships. A healthy substitute for expressing some of that "control" need is being in charge of our physical space and its appearance.

Whatever your physical space may be, keeping it clean, neat, and colorful will contribute immeasurably to reducing your stress.

Avoid "Skimming"

Because of the increased responsibilities and involvements of many women, they find themselves "skimming" in relationships. Rather than focusing on people, really listening, and being responsive, a woman will skim over the top of relationships. She only half hears what someone is saying. She may even avoid friends and family because she feels that she *doesn't have time* to relate. If the "skimming" continues, she will not only run the risk of alienating those close to her, she will also experience increased stress because her personal needs for support and affiliation will not be met.

As an active woman, you need to continually remind yourself of the importance of relationships. You don't necessarily need a lot of them, but certainly a breadth and diversity of relationships will remind you that first and foremost, you're a part of the human race! Olive Beech, Chairman of the Board of the Beech Aircraft Corporation, cautions, "Always leave enough time for your family and yourself *each day*."

Getting together with family and friends can be a spur-of-the-moment potluck supper or a Sunday brunch at a favorite restaurant. How about a long phone call on a rainy weekend afternoon . . . or even a long walk in the woods together? There are a multitude of ways to reconnect with those around you!

Beware of "skimming"—perhaps temporarily necessary, but never a long-term antidote to a busy schedule. Not only do those close to you need your psychological and physical presence, but you need theirs!

"What Am I Wanting That I'm Not Getting?"

One of the most common symptoms of stress is rebellious behavior. Whether fourteen years old or forty-four, we all have times when we feel rebellious inside and often will express it through childish and inappropriate behaviors. For example, have you ever been in a conversation with someone and the whole time the other person is talking to you, you're thinking, "I'm not going to do that! No way am I going to do that!"

Rebellion is often a symptom of stress and can be recognized as such. Also, understanding the rebellion is a potential tool in reducing the stress.

Whenever you realize you're feeling rebellious about something, ask yourself, *"What is it I'm wanting that I'm not getting?"* This question pulls you from your childlike state of rebellion into a more rational, problem-solving frame of mind. Often by asking that question, you will be able to figure out the source of the rebellious stress and begin to get a handle on resolving your problem.

If the phone has been ringing all morning while you've been trying to finish up the yearly action plan for your agency, then you're likely to be feeling frustrated and rebellious and probably will be communicating that negative message to the people at the other end of those telephone conversations. Stop for a minute and ask yourself, "Hey, what is it I'm wanting that I'm not getting?" You'll quickly realize that it's uninterrupted time to finish the action plan.

You can then decide to take the phone off the hook and finish the plan. Anyone needing to reach you will continue to call until the connection is made. Or, if your phone calls can be screened, messages can be taken and/or callback arrangements made.

Relish Your Senses!

How many of us go through days and even weeks without *really* seeing, hearing, smelling, tasting, touching. A common part of the "stress experience" is *not* being tuned in to our senses. We become so intent on racing from activity to activity with our minds crowded with "shoulds" and "have to's" that we literally "lose touch" with our environment.

A stress reducer and one that often requires *no extra time* is to train yourself to *really* see, hear, smell, taste, touch. This heightened awareness can occur during any portion of your daily routine.

Stop right now, and look around you at the variety of color within the reach of your vision. Concentrate on hearing all the sounds that are present. Are there one or more distinctive odors in the air? Be aware of the taste in your mouth. Run a finger of one hand up and down the sides of the fingers of your other hand. Five senses . . . a short one-minute sensual experience!

As you develop the habit of increased sensual awareness, you've provided an avenue for yourself to be more in touch with the natural flow of events and at the same time, reduced your level of stress.

Set Up a New Reward System

Many women create stress for themselves by believing that they can only "reward" themselves with leisure or a vacation by being a perfectionist in everything they do. *If* you meet all the demands of those around you, you *then* qualify for some treat for yourself—and *only then*. That's an unrealistic expectation to place on yourself and causes the kinds of stress-laden situations that need to be avoided.

A healthier and more caring approach to lessening your daily stress is to give up the "be perfect" expectations and devise a reward system which encourages and supports you. For example, you can reward yourself with a rose from the florist or a new scarf if you've completed one quarter of the project report or have only yelled at the children twice today—rather than waiting till you've completed the project or have somehow eliminated yelling from your repertoire of behaviors.

Reward yourself for achieving modest, short-term goals as well as the long-term. Remember that "you get what you stroke," a basic premise of behavior modification. Rather than hammering yourself over the head for not achieving some perfect goal, you need to give yourself a pat on the back for the progress you do make. When you make a mistake, give yourself a compliment for your awareness that a mistake was made, then play the situation back in your own head and determine how you can handle the situation differently should it occur again. In this process you are not only reinforcing your positive behavior, you're also literally creating for yourself a more confident and competent self-image.

The most important resource you have is yourself! Treat yourself with intelligence and affection—you deserve to be nurtured, supported, and cared for.

Finally, remember that every timewaster we've addressed contributes in one way or another to stress. As you manage your time, yourself, and your tasks more effectively, stress and tension will diminish and your life will be more satisfying and rewarding.

17

TIME FOR PLEASURE

Here is an hour . . . in which to think
  A mighty thought, and sing a trifling song,
    And look at nothing.

EDNA ST. VINCENT MILLAY (1920)

To take time for pleasure, time for herself, is a difficult assignment for many women. Caught up in the hectic pace of daily life, juggling varied responsibilities, and still abiding by many of the traditional "serve others" cultural messages, women often neglect their need to play, to have fun.

One example: Think of the typical weekend schedule for many men versus that for women. The man as a matter of course will spend part of his weekend hours at play, whether it's a game of golf or a few hours of beer and chitchat with his neighbor. The woman, however, is likely to spend the weekend getting caught up on the housework, chauffeuring the kids, and cooking mountains of food both for the weekend meals and also to freeze for the following week. Women typically spend far less time on the weekend engaged in leisure activities than do most men.

Your socialization as a woman with the expectation that you always are ready, willing, and available to meet the needs of others contributes immeasurably to the feeling of guilt that often results when taking time for yourself becomes the priority. Perhaps there is a lesson to be learned from men as you consider their attitudes and behaviors regarding play. Ann Richards, in reflecting on her busy life-style as wife, mother, and elected official, commented knowingly:

As far as advice for a twenty-year-old woman, I am staggered, thinking of my own child of that age. I suppose that I would suggest that she accept, without guilt, the notion that she cannot be everything to everyone. She must satisfy herself first, or she will not satisfy anyone. Having accomplished this mental revolution, she should know that women are different than men. Sociologically, women are taught to assume responsibility for making everything work as best it can, to take responsibility for the human costs and problems with every issue.

Men on the contrary, by the age of twenty have learned to play. They play with their work, viewing it as a form of sport. They play with their friends, on out-of-town hunting trips, community clubs or projects, or having a beer after work. They play at home with the children or with their wives. Team sports, a sense of the future in the notion of a career, and a belief that family is to be financially supported, but enjoyed, have traditionally contributed to this view.

Women on the contrary, make *everything* into work. Perhaps because we never valued our work as important in itself, we have transferred that same attitude toward the workplace. We make ponderous, backbreaking labor out of tasks that men would either get someone else to do, simply dispatch as a matter of course, or thoroughly enjoy. I do not think that we can admit yet, even to ourselves, that we enjoy the things that we do at work, that we enjoy the time we spend with friends at play, and do not intend to feel guilty about those attitudes.[1]

---

[1] Personal letter from Ann Richards.

Why is it important that you take time for yourself to relax and play? And even if it *is* important, how do you *find time* to do it?

Importance of "Fun" Time

Increasing research points to the importance of leisure activities for physical and psychological well-being. There is even a new career category of "leisure consultants," people who work with individuals and organizations to teach people how to incorporate more leisure activities into their lives.

All work and no play not only can make you dull, but can also cause you physical damage—whether it's high blood pressure or ulcers—while the psychological price may be a quick temper, sleepless nights, or worse. Think for a minute of what your physical and psychological symptoms are when you've not allowed yourself enough time for leisure. In almost every case, those symptoms will keep you from functioning as effectively as you might otherwise. How much better to avoid those symptoms by building in time for pleasure on a regular basis . . . and consequently being more productive in your work—all at the same time!

Finding Time . . . Your Responsibility

To make time for pleasure and fun is *not* a luxury, it's a responsibility you have to yourself! Just as you structure other facets of your life, work, family responsibilities, and so on, you also need to plan time for those leisure activities that give you pleasure. If tennis is your favorite form of relaxation, then just as you set up business appointments, you need to schedule tennis games—a week or two or even a month ahead. Get those dates on your calendar so that they are as firm as that upcoming dental appointment or placement interview. If you feel guilty scheduling in time for yourself, remember that you do have responsibility to keep yourself in top physical and mental condition!

As part of allowing yourself time for pleasure, you need to be able to say no to others. That may mean saying no to some of the demands that your spouse or children are making on you, or it may mean postponing taking on any additional church or civic responsibilities. There even may be times when, as you weigh the alternatives, you choose to turn down a special job assignment, knowing that it would place an unrealistic and unhealthy demand on your time and psyche. The bottom line needs to continue to be the maintenance of a healthy balance among the various aspects of your life, *including* leisure.

Lunchtime Leisure

Lunchtime is a favorite of many women for leisurely pursuits. Some women use their lunchtime to go to a nearby track to jog, others take a fast walk through a shopping center, while others take a few minutes to work on their current needlework project. Other leisurely lunchtime activities may include a tennis game, a workout in a gym, shopping for a piece of jewelry or a special cologne, visiting the library for a look at the latest books, strolling through a museum, having lunch in a tucked-away corner of your favorite restaurant, or reading your favorite magazine.

Wonderful Weekends

One of the most luxurious weekends for busy women is one in which no activities have been scheduled, other family members are gone, and you have your house or apartment to yourself. Even a few hours of this solitude can be rejuvenating. That time may be spent in "puttering around" the house, moving easily from one activity to the next, for once *not* preplanning what you're going to do. Several hours may drift by as you read from cover to cover that novel you've been wanting to read for months. Some women stay in bed all day, reading, writing letters, and contemplating.

Wonderful weekends for other women may include planning and giving a big dinner party or inviting all the children and grandchildren over for a volleyball or ping-pong tournament.

If it's done without time pressure or a "work mentality," a wonderful weekend may even mean several hours thinking through your current life-style and sense of direction. Where am I going? What are my projections for the future? A day or two of reflection coupled with jotting down your conclusions will be a major step toward the establishment of short- and long-range goals, followed by the setting of priorities related to those goals. Work can sometimes be play, too!

Fun at the Office?

Is it even possible to have fun at work? Is it appropriate to build into the work experience a sense of play? Much current psychological theory suggests that not only is it appropriate to bring some elements of play into the workplace, it enhances the effectiveness of that particular group or organization. In Transactional Analysis, there is the concept of an ego system in which each of us has parent, adult, and child ego states. Part of the child in you is your creativity, your inquisitiveness, your spontaneity, certainly positive attributes in most jobs. *If* the child in you feels that she is not welcome in a particular work environment, then the child will shut down . . . and your creativity and vibrancy are consequently not available to you.

How, then, is the child appropriately included in the work world? In more ways than we realize! Birthday cakes, betting on the World Series, coffee breaks, and telling jokes are all expressions of the child in us. Obviously, there are legitimate limitations to a childlike atmosphere in most organizations and businesses. It's important, though, to recognize the value of play even when we're working!

Words of Wisdom

In talking and corresponding with many women regarding their interest in time management, a frequent concern expressed was that of finding "time for pleasure." Some of those women are finding answers, and their thoughts are worth sharing.

"Plan your time with a holistic viewpoint," advises Lucia Landon, an active and vibrant contemporary woman. "Plan time for work and also schedule time to take care of your emotional and physical needs. Let there be a space in one's life often that opens itself up for spontaneous activities."

Shirl Brenneke, journalist, says, "Find out as early as you can when you're 'spending' your time and when you're 'investing' it. If you find you have 'time to waste,' waste it deliberately in something that recharges your inner batteries and refreshes you."

Travel can be a time solely for pleasure. Biz Greene remarks, "My traveling is for pleasure only, and I not only don't prioritize, I don't wear a watch. I just flow with what I want when I feel like it, for a change."

And finally, Mary Baird Acheson, artist and teacher, counsels, "I make a lot of lists, but one of my New Year's resolutions is not to let the lists *rule* me. Some days—don't wear a watch—don't make a list—just live. Look at the sunset and *feel* with all your pores. Laugh—love someone. Who's in charge of your life? is the key question."

MAKING IT STICK!

. . . if you want something very badly, you can
achieve it. It may take patience, very hard work, a real
struggle, and a long time; but it can be done. That
much faith is a prerequisite of any undertaking . . .

MARGO JONES (1957)

You've read about the philosophy and techniques of time
management for women. You've read the thoughts and suggestions of other women as they've dealt with the same
concerns. You're hopefully feeling a sense of excitement
and anticipation about implementing many of the different
approaches suggested. But how do you make it stick?

Even though you have a strong desire to see your work
habits improve, the best intentions are often shelved, and
plans implemented with enthusiasm do go astray for several
reasons. First, patterns of conduct are difficult to change,
and we fall back into our old habits with incredible ease.
Second, no definite and detailed plans are made, and no

actions are scheduled so that there are specific concrete things to do rather than vague intentions. And finally, considerable pressure is exerted from others to conform to the old habits and expectations, so that the easier path is to continue business as usual.

This need not be the pattern. Significant changes can occur. You *can* change your habits and markedly increase your time management effectiveness.

There are three factors that are essential to an effective application of time management to your life:

1. *Commitment to definite actions.* Unless your plans are specific and concrete it will be difficult to get them transferred into actual practice. General notions stay that way. Also, unless you are committed to put them into effect, nothing will happen. As with all habits, the first step is to *take clear, definite steps* to establish them.

2. *Continued, consistent effort.* A new habit needs practice and a firm stand against exceptions. Therefore you need to return periodically to *evaluate* your progress, note the lapses and failures, and initiate *corrective action* over a sufficient period of time so that habits are established. At least three months are needed, and probably a year is better, for this kind of evaluation and action.

3. *Group action.* Many of the failures are the result of external pressures from others—colleagues, co-workers, family members—other people's expectations that you will continue your former way of responding. To break these expectations, the best step is to get the commitment of others to be supportive of your efforts. Communicate your plans to those who will be affected by them and seek their agreement to respect them.

As specific follow-up suggestions to "make it stick," consider implementing the following time management process. It will reinforce and solidify many of the new concepts and techniques you've learned.

Time Management Process

First Day after Completing *About Time!*

Schedule the following activities during the first five days after completion of this book:

1. Time log for five days.
2. Team or boss-secretary timewaster profile (if applicable). Discuss, solve, and schedule the top-priority items.
3. Review actions to take to control your top three timewasters.
4. Plan time when you will be unavailable. (Quiet Hour)
5. Communicate plans of actions that affect relations with others.

During the First Week

1. Analyze log, and review priorities of timewasters.
2. At end of week review the progress you have made, what went wrong, and what you plan to do next week to correct it. (Progress—Problems—Plans)

One Month after Completing *About Time!*

1. Review the month's progress. Schedule actions to further control top three timewasters.
2. Review solutions to timewasters 4 to 6 and consider the steps to take. Schedule actions to solve each.
3. Reread parts of this book relating to the areas that you are working on. Use other time management resources to augment your study.

Two Months after Completing *About Time!*

1. Review the previous month's success. Schedule actions to further control timewasters.
2. Review the solutions to timewasters 7 to 10 and consider how to implement. Schedule actions to solve each.

Three Months after Completing *About Time!*

1. Take a time log. Analyze and compare this with the earlier ones.

2. On the basis of the log, estimate the time saved and the improved results on each of your ten top timewasters.
3. Identify those areas that now need emphasis.
4. Plan to solve, and schedule actions as before.

Long-Range Follow-up and Reinforcement

To avoid falling back into your old bad habits, to assist you in following up and in reinforcing sound time management practices, we have listed below some of the principal tools and techniques available to you.

1. *Time Log* taken:
    a. *Semiannually* to ensure against regressing into old habits; and
    b. *Occasionally,* to check up on a particular timewaster; or
    c. *Continually*, as a tool in exercising self-discipline by identifying the point at which one begins to waste time and immediately taking corrective action.
2. *Reviews* in which a few minutes are taken each month for a period of at least three months to review three elements of time management.
    a. *Progress*. What progress are you making in managing your time more effectively by controlling or eliminating your principal timewasters?
    b. *Problems*. What problems are encountered and how can they be solved?
    c. *Plans*. What plans have been made for continuing efforts to further enhance your effectiveness through improved time utilization?
3. *Reinforcement Programs and Materials*
    a. *Books and Articles*. Along with articles, books provide a rich source of reinforcing and expanding knowledge on time management. Those books with useful indexes or detailed tables of contents may be particularly

helpful in providing additional, quickly identifiable information on a particular subject

b. *Films*. Films are remarkably useful, both as introductions to a subject and as a means of portraying vividly some behavior which, otherwise, may be difficult to picture. Repetition of the same critical incident in a film permits in-depth analysis which may be very useful.

c. *Cassette Programs* with manuals designed for individual or group use. Beneficial as reinforcement for covering selected portions of the subject for review, discussion, and implementation.[1]

d. *Time Management Effectiveness Program*. A unique program consisting of twenty-four lessons to be used over a period of a year to aid in making effective use of the tools and techniques developed to control or eliminate your timewasters. Each lesson focuses upon one particular timewaster or expands the implementation and understanding of selected techniques and practices for a more effective utilization of time. It also provides an audit for personal effectiveness in each major timewaster area, thus enabling you to assess your individual progress or digression at regular intervals.[2]

What is the ultimate goal of improved time management? Why put forth the extra effort to change and grow? The answer may be deceptively simple.

To manage yourself and your time will enable you more fully "to laugh often and much, to win the respect of intelligent people and the affection of children; to earn the appreciation of honest critics and endure the betrayal of false

[1] Available through Alec Mackenzie and Associates, Inc., P. O. Box 130, Greenwich, N.Y. 12834.

[2] Available through Alec Mackenzie and Associates, Inc., P.O. Box 130, Greenwich, N.Y. 12834.

friends; to appreciate beauty, to find the best in others; to leave the world a bit better, whether by a healthy child, a garden patch or a redeemed social condition; to know even one life has breathed easier because you lived. This is to have succeeded."[3]

[3] Ralph Waldo Emerson, "Self-Reliance" (1841). Reprint (New York: Peter Pauper Press, 1967).

APPENDIX

The following is a sample of a typical woman's time log for the first few hours of her day. Notice particularly the "Comment/Disposition" column.

DAILY TIME LOG

Name:_____   Date: _____

Daily Goals: Deadline
(1) *Write up report*   *11:00*   (4) *Distrib. Mtg.,*
(2) *Report to S. K.*   *12:30*   *complete agenda*   *3:30*
(3) *Staff Mtg.,*   (5) *Catch up on*
       complete agenda   *2:00*   *correspondence*   *4:30*
                                             (6) _____ _____

PRIORITY: **1**—MOST IMPORT.; **2**—LESS IMPORT.; **3**—ROUTINE DETAIL;
4—LEAST IMPORT.

Time	Activity	Time Used	Prior.	Comment/Disposition
6:15	Showered and dressed	25		Could shower night before—more leisurely and relaxing then.
6:40	Prepared breakfast for family	20	3	Family members could share responsibility more.
7:00	Made bed and straightened house	20	1	Important for me to do because then I feel more organized and in control.
7:20	Cleaned up kitchen and put roast in slow cooker	15	2	Family members could each rinse their own dishes.
7:35	Drove to bank and deposited check	10	4	
7:45	Drove to office	15		Enjoy this time alone.
8:05	Read newspaper	20	4	Could read at lunch—first 20 minutes wasted.

Time	Activity	Time Used	Prior.	Comment/Disposition
8:25	*Read phone messages*	10		Could have secretary return some calls with information requested.
8:35	*returned call to B. R. re budget*	5	2	Good time to make calls; most in office at start of day.
	call to S. L. re budget meeting	5		" " "
8:45	*Got coffee, met Martha G.*	10	3	
8:55	*Opened, read mail*	25	3	Secty. could open, sort, and route mail, throw out junk mail.
9:00	*Dictated draft of report to secty.*	6	1	Not really organized. Needed decision from B. H. re: report.
9:26	*Called B. H.—Problem re: report*	8	1	
9:34	*Resumed dictation to secty.*	12	1	Dictating equipment would save time, mine and secretary's.
9:46	*Called S. K.—Quests. re: project*		2	

ANNUAL/MONTHLY OBJECTIVES
AND
WEEKLY WORK PLAN

Prior	Annual goals	Year	To Be Done In Month Of	Follow-up			
	1.						
	2.						
	3.						
	4.						
	5.						
	6.						
	7.						
	Monthly Goals	Month	To Be Done In Week Of				
	1.						
	2.						
	3.						
	4.						
	5.						

Weekly Work Plan

_____
Week

Projects	Mon.	Tue.	Wed.	Thurs.	Fri.
1.					
2.					
3.					
4.					
5.					
6.					

WEEKLY PLAN SHEET — 1

Priority	Phone	Week of _____ Meetings
	Write	Appointments
	Projects	Lunches

WEEKLY PLAN SHEET — 2

A. M. Mon. 10:00

_____
_____
_____
_____
_____

B. J. Mon. 11:00

_____
_____
_____
_____
_____

M. B. Tues. 10:00

_____
_____
_____
_____
_____

L. R. Tues. 11:00

_____
_____
_____
_____
_____

D. F. Wed. 10:00

_____
_____
_____
_____

P. C. Wed. 11:00

_____
_____
_____
_____

To schedule and list items for discussion with each person with whom you have regular contact, such as your boss, your team, and so on at a set time each week.

WRITTEN DAILY PLAN

Pri-ority	Objectives	Deadline
1.		
2.		
3.		
4.		
5.		

CHECKLIST FOR GETTING ORGANIZED

At Work

1. Keep yearly plan, 12 mos. ahead.

2. Keep weekly plan sheet.
3. Keep daily plan.

4. Use own priorities to say no to unreasonable requests.
5. Have secretary/assistant located to screen effectively.
6. Keep equipment and supplies most accessible.

7. Keep working files most accessible.
8. Use a filing system that works.
9. Use colored folders for urgent, to do, dictate, and review items.

10. Keep desk clear except for matter at hand.

11. Make sure all items have a proper place and are kept there.
12. Finish one task before starting another.

13. Delegate and keep paper where work is being done.

At Home

1. Plan housekeeping (yard-work, gardening, paint-ing) by months.

2. Keep weekly plan sheet.
3. Keep daily plan (especially if delegation involved.

4. Use priorities to rule out impracticable activities.

6. Keep equipment and supplies most accessible to job.
7. Have a desk or "office" located for optimum use.
8. Use a filing system that works.
9. Carry a notebook in purse for "to do's."

9½. Organize errands to save trips.
10. Keep things put away except for what working on.

11. Make sure all items have a proper place and are kept there.
12. Combine as many tasks as possible; i.e., washing and cooking, mending and TV viewing.
13. Delegate, and keep sup-plies, equipment handy for parts of house, specific jobs.

14. Screen paperwork. Have person screening:
    a. Handle it.
    b. Refer it.
    c. Postpone it but follow up.
    d. Expedite it.
15. Handle it once.
16. Enlist secretary/assistant to help keep desk clear.

17. Minimize filing. Practice wastebasketry.

18. Use form letters and speedimemos.

19. Reply on original.
20. Use tickler, follow-up, suspended file.
21. Use dictation equipment.

22. Update organization chart.

23. Update job descriptions.

24. Practice speed reading.

14. Screen mail. Toss anything possible immediately. Put rest into:
    a. Records file.
    b. Business or social "to do" places.
15. Handle it once.
16. Enlist husband/children to help keep house picked up. Organize child's room to make it easier for him.
    Enlist family members to take responsibility for areas, functions, of housekeeping, yardwork, gardening, etc.

17. Minimize picking up. Practice wastebasketry. Minimize filing. Practice wastebasketry.
18. Use bulletin board for family notes, reminders, messages.

21. If several children at home, walkie-talkie allows instant communication.
22. Use a revolving system for chores. Devise fair system that is accepted by members.
23. Update job descriptions as children get older.
24. Schedule family planning sessions on regular basis.

CHECKLIST FOR PLANNING MEETINGS*

It is so easy to forget some crucial items in the planning of meetings—some materials you wanted to be sure to have available, the telephone call to the custodian, the name tags, extra minutes of the last meeting, and many others. We have found it indispensable, and very embarrassment-preventing, to have a checklist to review and check off as part of the process of planning and leading meetings. The one on the following pages should be a good starter—one to add to, because all meetings, of course, are different, and all items are not relevant for every meeting. But in our experience the main headlines and most of the items are quite universal.

The checklist is organized under:

> Publicity Promotion Notifying
> Agenda and Resource Materials
> Responsibilities Before the Meeting
> Space Check-out
> Equipment for the Meeting
> Materials and Supplies for the Meeting
> Budget
> Income
> Just Before the Meeting
> At the Meeting
> End of Meeting—and After

CHECKLIST

Publicity/Promotion/Notifying	Who responsible	By when
_____notices—to whom	_____	_____
_____letters of invitation	_____	_____
_____directions to meeting place	_____	_____
_____phone calls	_____	_____
_____news releases	_____	_____
_____contact with the media	_____	_____
_____copies of speeches	_____	_____
_____copies of meeting plan	_____	_____

* From Eva Schindler-Rainman and Ronald Lippitt, *Taking Your Meetings Out of the Doldrums,* (The Association of Professional Directors, 40 W. Long St., Suite 1000, Columbus, Ohio 43215).

Publicity/Promotion/Notifying	*Who responsible*	*By when*
____pictures/photographs	_____	_____
____bulletin boards	_____	_____
____personal contacts	_____	_____
____other	_____	_____

Agenda and Resource Materials	*Who responsible*	*By when*
____copies of agenda	_____	_____
____contact people on the agenda	_____	_____
____materials needed (e.g., reprints)	_____	_____
____previous minutes	_____	_____
____committee reports	_____	_____
____previous agreement and time commitments	_____	_____
____others	_____	_____

Responsibilities Before The Meeting	*Who responsible*	*By when*
____leadership assignments	_____	_____
____documentation or recording assignments	_____	_____
____resource persons?	_____	_____
____observers?	_____	_____
____"hosting" roles	_____	_____
____making reports	_____	_____
____trying out equipment	_____	_____
____test whether charts, posters are readable	_____	_____
____test electrical outlets	_____	_____
____preview films for timing and content	_____	_____

Space Checkout

____size and shape of space   ____access to meeting room(s)
____electrical outlets   ____lighting

_____mike outlets
_____acoustics
_____doors
_____bathrooms (what, number can accommodate)
_____stairs
_____elevators
_____heat/cold regulation
_____ventilation
_____parking facilities: number and access
_____registration area
_____location
_____transportation, access to facility
_____room set-up arrangements

_____name of custodian/engineer, where to be reached
_____telephone access for messages and calling out
_____exhibit space
_____wall space for newsprints, etc.
_____emotional impact (color, aesthetics)
_____others
_____
_____
_____
_____
_____
_____

Equipment for the Meeting

_____tables (number, size, shape)
_____chairs (comfort, number)
_____microphones
_____audio tape recorder
_____audio tape cassettes
_____video tape recorder
_____extension cords
_____overhead projector
_____newsprint easel (chart stand)
_____slide projector
_____screen
_____platform
_____record player
_____records

_____gavel
_____coffee, tea dispensers
_____water pitchers
_____cups
_____camera
_____film
_____transparencies and appropriate pens and grease pencils
_____extension cords
_____ditto machine or other duplication equipment
_____film projector
_____chalkboard, chalk, eraser
_____typewriters
_____wastebaskets

Equipment for the Meeting

_____bulletin boards   _____others

_____pillows   _____

_____projection table(s)   _____

_____easel

Materials and Supplies for the Meeting

_____name tags/tents   _____copies of reports

_____small-tip felt pens   _____books

_____large-tip felt pens   _____visual aids

_____masking tape   _____puppets

_____paper clips   _____colored paper

_____crayons   _____pamphlets

_____pins   _____display materials

_____scissors   _____flowers or flower

_____stapler   arrangements

_____glue   _____decorations

_____newsprint paper   _____posters

_____scratch paper   _____instruction sheets

_____pencils   _____resumé of resource

_____ditto paper & ditto   people

        masters   _____directional signs (to

_____fluid for ditto masters   meeting

_____self-carbon paper   _____chalk (various colors)

_____reprints of articles   _____file folders

_____copies of previous   _____others

        minutes   _____

Budget

Costs   _Estimated cost_

_____mailing and stamps   _____

_____telephone calls   _____

_____telephone conferences   _____

_____rental of equipment   _____

_____rental of space   _____

_____paper materials   _____

        _____name tags   _____

        _____newsprint   _____

        _____paper   _____

        _____construction paper   _____

Budget

Costs   *Estimated Cost*

_____writing materials   _____

    _____pens   _____

    _____crayons   _____

    _____special pens for overhead _____

    _____grease pencils   _____

_____secretarial time   _____

_____transportation   _____

_____meals   _____

_____bar   _____

_____coffee, tea, juice   _____

_____folders   _____

_____tapes   _____

_____operator of projection equipment   _____

_____operator of P.A. equipment   _____

_____speaker fees   _____

_____consultant fees   _____

_____entertainment   _____

_____flowers   _____

_____film reproduction   _____

_____tape reproduction   _____

_____others   _____

_____   _____

_____   _____

                                                 Estimated
Income   *income*

_____registration fees   _____

_____sale of materials   _____

_____grants   _____

_____sale of meal tickets   _____

_____donations   _____

_____membership fees   _____

_____coffee and tea charges   _____

_____others   _____

_____   _____

_____   _____

	Who responsible
Just Before the Meeting	
_____seating arrangements—general session and subgroupings	_____
_____extra chairs	_____
_____extra tables	_____
_____P.A. system checkout	_____
_____equipment (easels, screens, etc.)	_____
_____materials (paper, pens, etc.)	_____
_____ashtrays	_____
_____water, glasses	_____
_____thermostat	_____
_____opening and closing of windows	_____
_____refreshment set-up	_____
_____registration set-up	_____
_____check that charts, boards, screens can be seen from everywhere	_____
_____agendas available	_____
_____other materials available for handouts	_____
_____name tags/tents	_____
_____table numbers	_____
_____coffee, tea, etc.	_____
_____evaluation forms ready	_____
_____reproduction equipment (e.g., ditto machine)	_____
_____audiovisual equipment ready	_____
_____others	_____
_____	_____
_____	_____

	Who responsible
At the Meeting	
_____meeting, greeting, seating of participants and guests	_____
_____documentation—recording	_____
_____greeting of latecomers	_____
_____evaluation activity	_____
_____handing out materials	_____

                                                          *Who
At the Meeting   responsible*

_____operation of equipment   _____

_____process review, stop sessions, etc.   _____

_____announcements   _____

_____others   _____

_____   _____

_____   _____

                                                          *Who
End of Meeting—and After   responsible*

_____collect unused materials   _____

_____return equipment   _____

_____clean up   _____

_____thank helpers   _____

_____read and analyze evaluation/feedback   _____

_____prepare feedback on feedback   _____

_____mail follow-up materials   _____

_____remind people of their follow-up   _____
          commitments—phone_____
                         write_____

_____lay plans for next meeting; date if there   _____
          is to be one

_____pay bills   _____

_____collect outstanding monies   _____

_____others   _____

_____   _____

A Few Ideas About the Use of This Checklist

For your own particular kinds of meetings you may want to create an abbreviated checklist. We suggest you reproduce whatever form is appropriate for you, making enough copies so that you and your co-workers can use one for each planning activity.

Then you will also have it available to hand to volunteers and other associates to whom you care to give help and support in their planning and leading of meetings.

CONFERENCE CALL AGENDA FORM

Checklist for Planned Telephone Conference
1. Give sufficient notice to all participants.
2. Send out agenda.
3. Send visual aids.
4. Appoint group leader at each location if required.
5. Advise conference operator 24 hours in advance.
6. Introduce participants.
7. Have questions and answers addressed to chairperson.
8. Appoint a secretary to take minutes of the meeting.

Checklist for Solving Urgent Problems
1. Bring in only those people who are essential.
2. Give conference operator the names, telephone numbers, and area codes. Tell the operator you wish a conference as soon as possible.
3. Introduce each participant.
4. Describe clearly the nature and urgency of the problem.
5. Ask each participant in turn for his or her contribution.
6. Make sure each participant knows what action is required of her or him by summarizing the results.
7. Take minutes of the meeting for future reference.

ROLES PEOPLE PLAY IN MEETINGS*

Group-Blocking Roles

The aggressor	Criticizes and deflates status of others; disagrees with others aggressively.
The blocker	Stubbornly disagrees; rejects others' views; cites unrelated personal experiences; returns to topics already resolved.
The withdrawer	Won't participate; "wool gatherer"; converses privately; self-appointed note-taker.
The recognition seeker	Boasts; talks excessively; conscious of his status.
The topic jumper	Continually changes subject.
The dominator	Tries to take over, assert authority, manipulate group.
The special-interest pleader	Uses group's time to plead his own case.
The playboy	Wastes group's time showing off; story-teller, nonchalant; cynical.
The self-confessor	Talks irrelevantly about his own feelings and insights.
The devil's advocate	More devil than advocate.

Group-Building Roles

The initiator	Suggests new or different ideas for discussion and approaches to problems.
The opinion giver	States pertinent beliefs about discussion and others' suggestions.
The elaborator	Builds on suggestions of others.
The clarifier	Gives relevant examples; offers rationales; probes for meaning and understanding; restates problems.
The tester	Raises questions to "test out" whether group is ready to come to a decision.
The summarizer	Reviews discussion; pulls it together.

Group Maintenance Roles

The tension reliever	Uses humor or calls for break at appropriate times to draw off negative feelings.

* From Hensleigh Wedgwood, "Fewer Camels, More Horses," *Personnel,* July–August 1967.

The compromiser	Willing to yield when necessary for progress.
The harmonizer	Mediates differences; reconciles points of view.
The encourager	Praises and supports others; friendly; encouraging.
The gate keeper	Keeps communications open; encourages participation.

INDEX

239

240